THE SECRET INNER ORDER RITUALS OF
THE GOLDEN DAWN

Some Other Titles From New Falcon Publications

Aha! The Sevenfold Mystery of the Ineffable Love   –Aleister Crowley
Bio-Etheric Healing   –Trudy Lanitis
Undoing Yourself With Energized Meditation and Other Devices
Secrets of Western Tantra: The Sexuality of the Middle Path
Dogma Daze
   –Christopher S. Hyatt, Ph.D.
Rebels & Devils; The Psychology of Liberation
   –Edited by Christopher S. Hyatt, Ph.D.
Aleister Crowley's Illustrated Goetia
Taboo: Sex, Religion & Magick
Sex Magic, Tantra & Tarot: The Way of the Secret Lover
   –Christopher S. Hyatt, Ph.D., and Lon Milo DuQuette
Pacts With The Devil
Urban Voodoo: A Beginner's Guide to Afro-Caribbean Magic
   –Jason Black and Christopher S. Hyatt, Ph.D.
The Psychopath's Bible
   –Christopher S. Hyatt, Ph.D., and Jack Willis
Ask Baba Lon   –Lon Milo DuQuette
Aleister Crowley and the Treasure House of Images
   –J.F.C. Fuller, Aleister Crowley,
   Lon Milo DuQuette and Nancy Wasserman
Enochian World of Aleister Crowley
   –Lon Milo DuQuette and Aleister Crowley
Info-Psychology
Neuropolitique
The Game of Life
What Does WoMan Want?   –Timothy Leary, Ph.D.
Rebellion, Revolution and Religiousness   –Osho
Reichian Therapy: A PracticalGuide for Home Use   –Dr. Jack Willis
Woman's Orgasm: A Guide to Sexual Satisfaction
   –Benjamin Graber, M.D., and Georgia Kline-Graber, R.N.
Shaping Formless Fire
Seizing Power
Taking Power   –Stephen Mace
The Illuminati Conspiracy: The Sapiens System –Donald Holmes, M.D.
An Insider's Guide to Robert Anton Wilson   –Eric Wagner
The Secret Inner Order Rituals of the Golden Dawn   –Pat Zalewski
Hinduism and Jungian Psychology
Sufism, Islam and Jungian Psychology   –J. Marvin Spiegelman, Ph.D.
Nonlocal Nature: The Eight Circuits of Consciousness
   –James A. Heffernan
on What is   –Ja Wallin

Other Titles by Dr. Israel Regardie

A Practical Guide to Geomantic Divination - A Small Gem
Attract and Use Healing Energy - A Small Gem
Be Yourself - A Guide to Relaxation and Health
Ceremonial Magic
Dr. Israel Regardie's Definitive Work on Aleister Crowley,
  The Eye In The Triangle
Healing Energy, Prayer and Relaxation
How To Make and Use Talismans - A Small Gem
My Rosicrucian Adventure
Teachers of Fulfillment
The Art and Meaning of Magic - A Small Gem
The Body-Mind Connection, A Path to Well-Being - A Small Gem
The Complete Golden Dawn System of Magic
The Eye in the Triangle: An Interpretation of Aleister Crowley
The Garden of Pomegranates
The Golden Dawn Audio CDs
The Legend of Aleister Crowley
The Magic of Israel Regardie
The Middle Pillar
The Philosopher's Stone
The Portable Complete Golden Dawn System of Magic
The Tree of Life
The Wisdom of Israel Regardie - Vol. I
  Selected Introductions, Prefaces and Forewords
The Wisdom of Israel Regardie - Vol. II
  Selected Essays and Commentaries
The Wisdom of Israel Regardie - Vol. III
  Selected Articles, Introductions, Prefaces and Forewords
What You Should Know About the Golden Dawn
Roll Away The Stone/The Herb Dangerous
  (Dr. Israel Regardie and Aleister Crowley)

MANY OF OUR TITLES AVAILABLE ON KINDLE!
Please visit our website at http://www.newfalcon.com

THE SECRET INNER ORDER RITUALS OF THE GOLDEN DAWN

By Pat Zalewski

Foreword by Dr. Tony Fuller

Preface by Martin Thibeault

Introduction by Pat Zalewski

NEW FALCON PUBLICATIONS
LAS VEGAS, NEVADA, U.S.A.

Copyright © 1988 by Patrick Zalewski

All rights reserved. No part of this book,
in part or in whole, may be reproduced, transmitted,
or utilized, in any form or by any means, electronic or mechanical,
including photocopying, recording, or by any information storage
and retrieval system, without permission in writing
from the publisher, except for brief quotations
in critical articles, books and reviews.

ISBN 13: 978-1-56184-535-4
ISBN 10: 1-56184-535-3

First Published Edition 1988
Second Revised Edition New Falcon 2016

The paper used in this publication meets the minimum requirements
of the American National Standard for Permanence of
Paper for Printed Library Materials Z39.48-1984

Printed in USA

NEW FALCON PUBLICATIONS
9550 South Eastern Avenue • Suite 253
Las Vegas, NV 89123
www.newfalcon.com
email: info@newfalcon.com

TABLE OF CONTENTS

Foreword	Dr. Tony Fuller	1
Preface	Martin Tribeault	5
Introduction	Pat Zalewski	9
CHAPTER 1	Felkin and the New Zealand Order	11
CHAPTER 2	The Origins of the Rosicrucian Order	47
	The Cypher Manuscripts	59
CHAPTER 3	The Gods and Rituals	93
CHAPTER 4	Enochian Pronunciation	119
	The Magical Language: "A Vocabulary"	123
CHAPTER 5	The 6=5 and 7=4 Rituals of the R.R. et A.C.	143
APPENDIX I	The Equinox Ceremony	203
APPENDIX II	The Portal of the Rosy Cross	213
APPENDIX III	Inner Order Study Curriculum	239
APPENDIX IV	"The Order of the Round Table	243

FOREWORD

THE LAST OUTPOST OF THE GOLDEN DAWN

For any modern scholar of the history of that extraordinary Victorian magical Order known as the Hermetic Order of the Golden Dawn Pat Zalewski's *Secret Inner Order Rituals of the Golden Dawn* was groundbreaking. Indeed it was also particularly exciting for all those modern occultists who in the 1970s began to use published rituals and teachings to revive the Order. Pat's book appeared in 1988 and not merely provided hitherto unknown rituals and papers but also provided the first public exposure of the astonishing news that in remote New Zealand a Temple which had opened in 1912 had continued to operate in secrecy right up until late 1978.

The Temple was formally titled Smaragdum Thalasses and was the very last remaining temple of the Hermetic Order of the Stella Matutina, an immediate and direct descendent of the short-lived Golden Dawn. To say it was the last to close its doors and cease functioning is not a metaphorical description for, unique amongst all the temples, Smaragdum Thalasses possessed its own architecturally designed building, named 'Whare Ra' or 'House of the Sun', which was constructed for the express purpose of conducting the magical ceremonies of the Order. The curtain call came on 24 August 1978 when a letter was sent to all members from the three Chiefs announcing the closure and the fact that there would be 'no Vernal Equinox ceremony'. In their letter they state; *"The Chiefs have very reluctantly reached the conclusion that the Order, at least in its present form, has served its purpose and the Divine Guardians have withdrawn themselves."*

With a membership of between 300-400 men and women throughout its relatively untroubled and secret lifespan of 66 years, it was clearly the most successful of all the Golden Dawn temples. But not until Pat's book emerged ten years after closure was anything known about Whare Ra other than a few brief references found in a number of books written by various authorities on the Order history. Indeed, as late as 1986 Dr. R. A. Gilbert writes, with regard to the temple, that *'after 1916...nothing further is known of its history'*. Over a period of nearly 30 years since the publication of *Secret Inner Order Rituals of the Golden Dawn* a growing body of literature has arisen concerning this extraordinary temple–many also written by Pat–and it is attracting increasing attention from scholars around the globe.

What made Pat's book unique within this historical field was that many members of the temple were still alive and Pat was able, through personal friendships and shared interests, to speak directly to them and obtain contemporary accounts of their experiences. In this regard my own personal history has a curious parallel with Pat's. Quite independently of him I became closely acquainted with many of the Whare Ra members and with all its last Chiefs. And it was just after Pat had published this important book that I met him and we have remained close friends ever since, comparing and exchanging our own often different experiences of working with Whare Ra members. Precisely because of the longevity of the temple, its large membership and many surviving documents, the historical narrative of Smaragdum Thalasses is extremely rich and thus through our different access to individuals and documents we were each frequently able to acquire information not available to the other. I am delighted that Pat and *New Falcon Publications* have reissued an updated edition of this groundbreaking book. Although we now know far more about the history of the Order and this temple in the years which have passed since its first publication, the book is in no way outdated and it remains as valuable to the scholar and occultist as it ever was. And for this we owe a debt of gratitude to Pat for having the foresight to ensure that firsthand impressions and knowledge of some of the Order's last members are recorded for posterity.

Tony Fuller
October 2016

PREFACE

When this book was first published in 1988, its author Pat Zalewski was a name known only to very few in the Golden Dawn community at large. In fact, the community itself was still very small and fragmented. Nevertheless, the contents of the book were extremely impactful because they made available for the first time some very advanced teachings of the Order. Among these were the 6=5 Adeptus Major and 7=4 Adeptus Exemptus Initiation Ceremonies of the Stella Matutina's Inner Order, which had nowhere else before been published. In addition to these and certainly no less important, was the publication of Flying Roll 39– The Etheric Link. This flying roll contains a powerful ceremony which passes on an R.R. et A.C. lineage, and which only a handful of us in the world today have received and have the ability to transmit.

The new release of this book is a most welcome addition to every Golden Dawn practitioner's library for it is not only a classic in the field, but now comes with many major additions and corrections. Pat Zalewski, a Magus 9=2 with 40+ years of experience in the G.D.'s 1st, 2nd, and 3rd Orders, has decided to come forward and unveil some of the blinds and omissions from the previous edition and to include further relevant historical information in the new chapter on 'Felkin and the New Zealand Order'. With both the 6=5 and 7=4 now complete and the Enochian Dictionary copy being a more extensive one, we have Dr. Tony Fuller to thank for providing additional copies for a comparative study.

For all serious students of the Golden Dawn tradition, this book is a gemstone not only for some of the rare and hitherto unpublished material it contains, but also because of the knowledge and experience its author shares when introducing these. Pat Zalewski's impact on the modern manifestations of the Golden Dawn is something which is generally understated. Being one of the very few remaining Adepti who have been properly trained by Adepti from the old Order, his understanding of the tradition far exceeds anything which most Order heads and G.D. authors of today would dream of. I am not saying this to make diminishing comparisons, but rather to accentuate the wonderful opportunity all of us Golden Dawn students have in being able to continue to tap into the wealth of experience and knowledge of a teacher such as Pat Zalewski.

Publications as these are few and far between, and they are of tremendous value for our Great Work. I personally have the honour and pleasure of having Pat as an Initiator, Mentor, Brother, and Friend, and I simply cannot express enough how blessed we are to have him leading the way in this powerful Golden Dawn system which is so vast and intricate. I can only hope that I too, being his sole successor and the main carrier of his teachings, will like him be able to shine as a beacon of light for our Egregore. Our community of varying Golden Dawn Orders who share in the mysteries benefit tremendously through books such as the one you are holding. In fact, amidst all of our differences in culture and method, it is the knowledge both oral and written which unites us in the spirit of our work. Let us always remember this and may this book prove to be both of value to our personal work as individuals, as well as to our Order and its work as a whole.

Martin Thibeault
9°=2° K.'.R.'.

Archon Basileus of the
Order of the Golden Dawn

OrderoftheGoldenDawn.com

INTRODUCTION

The idea to publish this book originally came through a frustration with Golden Dawn authors stating that all the Golden Dawn temples had closed their doors by the end of the 1950s and that Israel Regardie was the last living adept of the Golden Dawn. From that point the concept of an imagined Golden Dawn began to form in some authors' minds as to what they taught and how they taught, solely based on papers without any context for knowing how those papers were delivered, what the teachings were and with a lack of understanding what the oral traditions were. Temples were springing up like mushrooms in cow paddock and those that wanted to explore above the 5=6 were using Waite's modified rituals and some of Crowley's. The only way to help change this was to publish these higher Stella Matutina rituals and create a level playing field by providing everyone with the 6=5, 7=4 and Etheric link rituals. Regardie had published the rituals up to 5=6 and I wanted to round it off with this publication. At that point I had not anticipated writing anything more other than to let people know what we had in New Zealand so the Whare Ra history would be more than a footnote. Whatever my intention was, fate apparently had something else in mind for me. Before I was going to publish the rituals, I felt I had to ask permission from some of my ex Whare Ra seniors and got their blessing to do so.

The second edition would never have seen daylight if it was not for Tony Fuller, who had many of the same experiences I had with ex Whare Ra members. He convinced me to correct a number of errors in the book, especially in the rituals and also sharpen up some of the Whare Ra history and add more information in that area. Tony is currently writing his own book on Whare Ra history and I see this second edition as preamble to what is to come from him which will be quite considerable.

Pat Zalewski

CHAPTER 1

FELKIN AND THE NEW ZEALAND ORDER

If ever there was a character straight from the pages of a Rudyard Kipling novel then Dr. Robert Felkin would be a most likely candidate. A medical missionary in Africa and expert in tropical diseases who spurred on towards African missionary work by meeting with explorer David Livingston who gave a lecture at his grammar school in England. The British medical journal of February 12th, 1926 gives an interesting snapshot of Felkin's life as a missionary in his obituary. Some of his more flamboyant adventures with equally flamboyant characters were when Felkin met General Gordon at Khartoum, just before his death, and further on with Mehmed Emin Pasha, an Ottoman-German physician, naturalist, and governor of the then Egyptian province of Equatoria (now Southern Sudan and upper Uganda) on the white Nile. The journey from the Nile to the Great Lakes was fraught with danger and hardship, but eventually Felkin and his companions reached Uganda. In February, 1879, he was presented to King M'tesa, and became his personal physician. Felkin was challenged by an

Dr. Robert Felkin

anti-missionary movement with the tribes which placed him and his party in great danger which he only survived by predicting an eclipse and established his bone fides as power medicine man. This was some six years before Kipling wrote of such an event in *King Solomon's Mines*, which also took place in the general Uganda area. Felkin may have been the inspiration for that passage that Kipling relied on. Much of his time in Uganda was spent in the study of local diseases, and he also made anthropological measurements of the pygmies. He left Uganda with the envoys of King M'tesa to Queen Victoria, and returned with them safely to the Nile, thus destroying an old superstition that no white man could journey to the Great Lakes and back without losing his life. His next expedition was to Zanzibar, where he lived for three years and worked with the explorers Schweinfurth, Buschta, Junker, and Sir Harry Johnston. His interest in the welfare of the natives made him a strong opponent of the slave trade, and he became a very active member of the Anti-Slavery Society. During his time in Africa he claimed to have witnessed many incredible events such as a caesarean birth delivering by local tribesman in 1879 and a transfiguration–the process of animals appearing out of thin air through the power of a witch doctor.

Dr. Felkin joined Amen Ra Temple of the Golden Dawn in Edinborough in March 1894 and by December 1896 he was admitted to the Inner Order along with his first wife Mary. By 1900, Felkin was an influential member of the Hermetic Golden Dawn's Inner Order and prominent member of the Sphere Group which delved into Enochian research. The split in the Golden Dawn came in 1900 when Samuel Mathers accused fellow Chief, Dr. Wynn Westcott of fabricating the orders' esoteric and historical origins which resulted in schism in the order. One group under Mathers renamed their order as the Alpha et Omega which the second group who retained the bulk of the Golden Dawn membership still maintained the original name until 1902 and ran itself by committee with elected Chiefs, Felkin being one of them alongside Brodie Innes and Percy Bullock and the name of the order was changed to Morgen Rothe. At that time Dr. Felkin was known for his clairvoyant ability and aided by his second wife who was equally well versed and claimed contact with entities called the Sun Masters and who claimed to be connected to the Golden Dawn's Third Order, exactly what it entailed was never a clear point other than a high level of adeptship.

In 1903 a further split developed in the Golden Dawn with A.E. Waite's group rewriting the rituals and decidedly were not looking for astral masters which was the primary point of philosophical difference between the two groups. Felkin believed in astral masters and SDA connection to the Golden Dawn and was actively looking for them in the flesh or otherwise, while clearly Waite did not. The Felkin–Waite relationship was an uneasy alliance of sorts with both groups sharing the original Golden Dawn papers. Waite was their custodian which continued up until the First World War. It was something Felkin later regretted when Waite refused to hand over any of those documents when he asked for them. Both groups at this point had different names with The Stella Matutina under the Felkin, Innes and Bullock triad and the Holy Order of the Golden Dawn under Waite.

By the late 1980s and for most occult historians the Golden Dawn had ceased to exist by 1900 with the highest studied grade attained being the second subgrade of the 5=6, the Theoricus Adeptus Minor plus nominal 6=5 and 7=4 grades. Mathers, Woodman and Westcott were the nominal 7=4 and Moina Mathers had reached the 6=5 level. Also there has been no indication of any advanced papers beyond the level of Theoricus Adeptus Minor and some of those appear to have been written post 1900 even though the list of documents for those levels were written pre-1900, which is a puzzle in itself.

At that stage, there were subgrades within the Adeptus Minor level of which only two were worked: Zelator Adeptus Minor and Theoricus Adeptus Minor. A third subgrade of Practicus Adeptus Minor was drafted up although it was never implemented within the Golden Dawn's Inner Order: the Rosea Rubea et Aurea Crucis. The final subgrade of Adeptus Adeptus Minor was in fact never utilized in the Golden Dawn proper.

In approximately 1898, an American couple by the name of Lockwood, who were members of the small Ahathoor Temple Mathers ran in Paris, were reported to have been advanced to the level of Adeptus Exemptus, or the 7=4 grade. Many considered this grade a nominal one, based on the Mathers relationship with his English temples. This point made by Paul Foster Case is a mystery that is not fully resolved unless those levels were nominal only as no papers beyond the 5=6 level were passed onto the American temples. Only Moina Mathers at that time was advanced to the level of 6=5 and it's highly unlikely that the Lockwoods would have been promoted above her. Apparently, what Mathers had done in Ahathoor was to do away with the subgrades of the 5=6 grade and adopt a version of the Theoricus Adeptus Minor. In post 1900 there is scant reference to these subgrades except by Brodie Innes. It is highly likely that he placed his own material in the 5=6 curriculum, slightly enlarged that was issued to his British temple.

During the next seven years Felkin came under increasing pressure to make a connection with the fabled Golden Dawn's Mother Temple Litch, Libe, Und Leben. Part of this pressure was for entrance to the higher levels and material for them. However it was Felkin's confident and close friend Neville Meakin who made the initial breakthrough when he paved the way for Felkin to go to Europe with his Rosicrucian contacts. Meaken was admitted to the Stella Matutina in April 1909 and by January 1910 he was promoted to 5=6. A very short time frame of just ten months. It appears the customary wait period between grades was ignored in this instance for political expediency and a dash of nepotism on the part of Felkin, and also Waite, who also wanted to settle the argument of the original Golden Dawn connection in the hope that Meakin might find something out. It was Waite who claimed giving him the 5=6 grade at Basset Road and also an acting 7=4 so he could deal with the European Rosicrucians. Considering the very short time frame of admittance to the order and his death, some three years later, Meakin's work in the order can only be classed as extraordinary and far reaching and he is very underrated in general by Golden Dawn historians. It was primarily Meakin that altered the original Golden Dawn Portal ritual where all the diagrams were placed in the east for the Stella Matutina version which had them placed around the temple in a balanced manner in keeping with the original pattern.

Once the European Rosicrucian contacts were established by Meakin, it was just over 12 months before Felkin left for Europe. Meakin, who laid the infrastructure for Felkin to visit Steiner, died in 1912 of tuberculosis. Felkin, with his wife and daughter, visited Germany the same year and met with Steiner who was at that time the most visible head of the Rosicrucian movement on the continent with a reputation also as a healer. One of the driving forces behind Felkin's European contact appears to be his belief in a literal Christian Rosenkreutz–and not as an allegory. When Felkin returned to England he claimed the equivalent of 8=3, through his continental connections, which was one step higher than Mathers and Westcott who had made similar claims. To the best of my knowledge modern scholars have not got to the bottom of what Steiner gave Felkin. Felkin's diary notes claim he was admitted to some group and obtained the 8=3 for himself and lesser ranks for his wife and daughter. On the face of it, to a certain extent justifies his claims, but what he was actually initiated into is obscure. Most historians accept that Felkin's 8=3 was an equivalency and not an actual 8=3, as there was no direct Golden Dawn connection to make it so. However, the equivalency soon became an actuality, with the writing of the higher grade rituals by Felkin up to the level of 9=2. The most likely scenario is a simple one and that is because Steiner and his group gave him recognition as head of a Rosicrucian order in his own right and it is seriously doubted that Steiner issued any direct grades to Felkin, but with recognition (most likely a ceremonial one), came status as being the link to Rosicrucian Europe (through Steiner) which was like a blank cheque for Felkin to have total control.

There was an order that was established in the 1890s that many of the original Golden Dawn temples members including Mathers, Brodie Innes and Felkin joined and that was the Sun Order, which had established the Cromlech Temple. For the most part this order's significance had flown under the proverbial radar except for an outing of some of its papers by Francis King in his 1971 publication *Astral Projection, Ritual Magic and Alchemy*. Brodie Innes became a leading light in this order and it is unclear if he wrote a number of their auric papers or inherited them, with the latter being more likely the case.

What is clear is that Mathers had some sort of involvement in this and had been a member of this order from the 1890s. Part of this is indicated when Felkin returned to England around 1913 and started up a correspondence with Brodie Innes who had deserted the Stella Matutina for the Alpha et Omega group under Mathers. Brodie Innes replied:

"I have stacks of MSS., and teachings going to far further than lengths than I used to think possible…"

Among these teachings were the elusive 6=5 and 7=4 grade rituals that had for so long been dangled as a carrot to Golden Dawn members and yet were now available for those who chose to work with Mathers. It would take a great deal of imagination to agree with this, with what has been published on post 1900 ritual and papers of Mathers to class them as Brodie Innes had done. However, if the Cromlech Temple auric papers are involved collectively, then Brodie Innes is being truthful. The puzzling part of this reply to Felkin is that Brodie Innes is referring to Mathers as an overall source for these documents and as if he had not seen them before. Perhaps he was not on the highest Cromlech levels where these were made available. The question to ask is what level did Golden Dawn members reach who joined it? It appears that Mathers had little left to give and these papers certainly fitted the bill for what he needed as a carrot. These Cromlech Temple papers were so integrated into Alpha et Omega highest levels that even Moina Mathers chastised Paul Case for revealing too much until she was told he had not received them as he was not above old 5=6 level where these papers were given out.

Once Felkin knew that Mathers was now dispensing the higher level grades with material for them he had to act and in a short time produced the rituals which were modifications of what Steiner gave him, from masonry and also from his inner plane contacts. Not to be outdone, he created rituals for Daath, Binah and Chockmah which were the Babe of the Abyss, Magister Templi and Magus. These were three higher levels than Mathers created. It certainly placated the unrest in some Stella Matutina temples though eventually he had to face up to what to put in each level and that was placed onto the too hard basket. Felkin played to his strengths and that was to claim a high level teacher who was above the Golden Dawn and not part of it. Steiner fitted the bill but with the looming First World War and frenzied anti-German sentiment being whipped up by the press at the start of the war in 1914 it was hard to keep Steiner in the picture. Also Steiner was in the middle of changing his alliances as well.

Due to the impact of Theosophy, there was a general trend towards eastern mysticism and that usually meant something of Indian origin. One person who was very important in Felkins' life and also that of many other Golden Dawn luminaries was a former Solicitor General of Ceylon, Sir Ponnambalam Ramanathan, Knight of the British Empire, who was an associate of Colonel Olcott co-founder of the Theosophical Society.

Sir Ponnambalam Ramanathan

Ramanathan was well-known to Alan Bennett whom he supported when he went to then Ceylon to study Buddhism and also Crowley who studied with him for a time in Ceylon. His arrival in England around 1913 coincided with a major social change of accepting Indian mystics as teachers and was vanguarded by Tagore winning the noble prize in literature. Yeats, Florence, Farr, Bennett and Crowley all considered Ramanathan to be a master par excellence in esoteric matters. When Florence Farr left England she went to teach at Ramanathan's school for girls in the north east of Ceylon, a country she never left.

Whatever his shortcomings, Felkin was a remarkable individual and had more than one teacher, whether astral or in the flesh. A good example of this is illustrated in his diary notes written around 1913 which were later published as a biography entitled *The Wayfaring Man*. The following is an extraction from it:

> "Not very long after he had left, we had another visitor of a very different stamp, my revered Teacher Sri Parananda [Ramanathan]; I think we all regarded it as an immense honor when he consented to come and stay with us... my first meeting [with Ramanathan] took place in a rather curious way. One year when Janey and I were at Bad Prymont, I was having my bath, lying in the delicious hot water and watching the steam rising in the pleasantly dreamy state that these baths induce, when I saw the head and shoulders of a man forming in the steam. I had the wit to lie perfectly still and passive, and by degrees I had made out a dark eastern face with a beard and large black eyes. The man was wearing a peculiar conical

cap, not a turban, and the steam appeared to be forming the outline of flowing robes. As I gazed, hardly daring to breathe, a voice came to me saying "One month from today I will meet you in London. Go to the lounge of the Carlton Hotel and wait for me."

A month later, punctually at three o'clock, I entered the lounge of the Carlton Hotel and looked about me. There was no bearded Oriental there, to my great disappointment and I sat down to wait. Ten minutes later, a quiet, slender Indian gentleman, clean shaven, turbaned, and wearing a black surtout buttoned to the neck, came down the stairs. I watched him anxiously and it seemed to me that the eyes and brow were those in the vision. He glanced around and came and sat near me. After a moment's hesitation, I leaned forward and said to him, "Excuse me addressing you, but if you wore a beard and cap I should say that I have been told to meet you here."

He looked at me with a pleasant smile and said, speaking in the somewhat careful clipped English of an Eastern, "Where was it that you saw me thus?"

"Exactly a month ago."

"At that time I was travelling in the mountains of Ceylon and I did indeed wear a cap and a beard. You are perfectly right; let us go to my private sitting room where we can talk quietly."

Thus began one of the most valued friendships of my whole life. Parananda was a Shivite Hindu by birth; a highly educated, cultured man, whether judged by Eastern or Western standards. A lawyer by profession, he became Solicitor

General of Ceylon not long after this meeting. He used his great talents and high position to alleviate the lot of his fellow countrymen, and raise the standard of education for both boys and girls...Looking back over our intercourse, I find it difficult to explain wherein his great influence lay. It was not anything he said or did so much as his whole attitude to life.

In his book *Magicians of the Golden Dawn*, Ellic Howe gives very little information on the U.S. temples which had a membership said to equal that of their British counterparts. Around 1910, Felkin received a series of small white books from Waite containing the Outer Order rituals and the Equinox of the Holy Order of the Golden Dawn. These, according to Waite, were "newly constructed from the Cipher Manuscripts, and issued by the authority of the concealed superiors of the Second Order, to members of recognized Temples." On comparing these with the Golden Dawn rituals, they are almost identical as far as structure goes, with Waite using his own invocations. Waite was working Golden Dawn rituals which differed only slightly in structure from those practiced in the Alpha et Omega and Stella Matutina. One interesting point is Waite used the Mather's cards in the rituals, though his own pack was then published.

Dr. Tony Fuller's patient scholarship unearthed an astonishing turn of events while studying Wynn Westcott's diary entries. In July 1915, Felkin's former Chief, and co-founder of the Golden Dawn, took from Felkin the Adeptus Major grade due to his continental Rosicrucian connections. Apparently the 7=4 grades that Mathers and Westcott assumed were nominal grades only. It was Felkin who provided Westcott with rituals for those levels and by July 1916 he was promoted to the rank of 8=3. These were apparently small ceremonies as the Stella Matutina temples had closed their door during the First World War. Westcott's actions here are very telling for they indicate that Westcott accepted Felkin's higher European Rosicrucian connections out of hand which in turn opened the door for his claimed Soror SDA connections as being fraudulent. The hope by Felkin that Westcott would head a Stella Matutina group soon evaporated with Westcott's departure to South Africa in 1920.

During the ten years that Felkin lived at Whare Ra he ran the temple like a military operation. Classes were held on week nights for Outer Order members in which esoteric philosophy and ritual were taught. On weekends he held classes for the Inner Order members to hone their knowledge to a fine point. These included ritual, Enochian pronunciation, and meditative exercises in the vault. By 1926, the year of Felkin's death, the Inner Order had grown to over 100 members with an unspecified number in the Outer Order. The Inner Order group was an extremely wealthy one and had members in many of the key local bodies throughout the Havelock North and Hastings area and collectively wielded a tremendous amount of power for the area. Some felt this when they tried to divulge information on Whare Ra to outsiders. One such individual (whose wife was apparently a member) was convinced that Felkin practiced black magic in his basement and was determined to close the temple down. He went to a number of local bodies and authorities to have him stopped. Needless to say, the individuals he approached on these committees were all Whare Ra members who "persuaded" him, after "thorough investigations" that his actions were unjustified.

Over the years there has been a great deal written how the Golden Dawn taught their members based on archival papers which barely has scratched the surface on temple teaching methodologies. At Whare Ra, a very elaborate process of teaching was established. The person in charge would be the daemonstrator who had regular monthly and bi-monthly meetings with students to check up on their progress. The general area of Whare Ra constituted two cities, Hastings and Napier and then a general rural area dotted with numerous small towns and a large number of orchards and farms. The area was a large one and was divided up into various sections under temple wardens, whose job was to help with the teachings in the local areas on a regular basis that filled in the period monthly and bi-monthly temple visits. The third tier to this which often overlapped with second tier wardens was when temple members had a mentor to help them further. In the heyday of the temple I believe there were five wardens and an undisclosed number of mentors, who were usually Inner Order members.

To give an example, the small town of Taradale, within the Whare Ra rural area boundaries, produced a number of high ranking Adepts. Depending on the time line involved, Taradale would be under a warden who lived in the town and at a later period would be under a warden who lived in a nearby area. In the 1950s there were at least one 8=3 and five or six 7=4s plus about five people of 6=5 and unknown number of 5=6s and Outer Members living in the town and surrounding area. This was the pool of expertise that members could draw on as many of them would mentor lower ranked temple members in a tight knit community. What made this more complex was due to the fact that many temple members had not seen a temple study curriculum apart from some core papers, some of which were attached to their temple ritual books. The wardens and some mentors often wrote their own study papers but as an adjunct to basic core teachings. When members would officially be called to temple to be instructed by the daemonstrator for their particular grade level, they would have had regular coachings and on all manner of subjects including mock rituals. This is then overlaid with those who sought special instruction for subjects such as Enochian work would often meet as groups, regardless of where you lived. For example Percy Wilkinson who lived in Napier had to travel long distances south of Hastings to meet up with Hugh Campbell and a small group who were then instructed in and played Enochian chess. There were many more groups such as this on all manner of subjects.

The manner on how people were taught or the general influence was that everything, I mean everything, came back to ritual analysis and this was done through layers of meaning which often interacted with other aspects of the Golden Dawn teachings. On the higher end of this scale many of them used a study of chakras and subtle bodies to explain what was happening in ritual. Some of these observations were very elaborate. I can remember vividly on one occasion sitting down with Evonne Salt, former wife of Frank Salt, whose favourite ritual office was Hegemon, something she had held for many years. After a three hour conversation with her I found out a wealth of information about the position, the problems she had with members, and the polarity that she observed. The amount of information she gave out was unbelievable and covered a complete range. This was the old way on how they taught based on personal experience and not just book learning.

Within recent years, some occult historians have accused Felkin of being a deluded dreamer, and an individual who sanctioned "astral junketing." Having met people who knew Felkin in New Zealand, a totally different person emerges than that portrayed by historians. Firstly, he was a perfectionist who demanded a great deal of his students. Secondly, he was a down to earth individual. The "astral junketing" of those in the Amoun Temple never occurred at Whare Ra; of this I have been assured by a number of Whare Ra members from the Temple's early days. If Felkin was a dreamer, as Ellic Howe claims, it was a totally different man who came to New Zealand, for he must have undergone a dramatic change in character.

One of the major problems that caused Whare Ra to split from the Stella Matutina was the buildup of insane comments to the Felkins from the Amoun Chiefs. The Stella Matutina temples had a certain amount of autonomy and in the late 1920s Bristol Temple started cutting rituals down as shown by what Regardie first published. Within the Inner Order of the Stella Matutina in the Outer, there is a great deal of astral work too involved not to be undertaken without using the prescribed Order safeguards. Failure to do so could result in the practitioner encountering the same problems experienced by Amoun Chiefs, as Francis King relates in his book, *Ritual Magic in England*. Felkin, on the other hand, had strict rules about skrying, and often preached about the dangers of over-skrying (i.e. too much too often in a limited period).

Without doubt, the most forgotten of all the Golden Dawn temples was Whare Ra, yet it was described by those who had seen others as the largest in size and membership.

The Official Whare Ra History lecture is as follows:

"After Ruth and Reginald Gardiner arrived from Canada, they settled in Havelock North, a small village in the East Coast District of the North Island of New Zealand, in 1907, where his brother, Rev. Allen Gardiner was vicar. They met an old friend—Harold Large—who had just left the Theosophical Society and been confirmed by the Bishop of Auckland. He did this because he considered the Eastern training unsuitable for Western people and was convinced that there must be esoteric training somewhere in the West.

He inspired the Gardiners with his enthusiasm for this quest, and during his two year stay they developed time daily in prayer and meditation to this purpose.

The group of three were soon joined by Miss Mary McLean, a trained teacher from Scotland, and Miss Gardiner who had been trained as a kindergarten teacher at Sesame House, London.

Miss McLean was acquainted with Dr. Carnegie Dickenson, a former Chief of the Amen-Ra Temple, and had met Father Fitzgerald and was imbued with the same idea as Harold Large. H.L. assisted the sympathetic and helpful vicar as lay reader, and being a trained organizer with dynamic enthusiasm, built round this silent power station a cultural society which was given the name of "Havelock Work" (Havelock North being the name of the village they were in). It's purpose being to encourage the talent of the musical, dramatic, and literary people who were attracted to it.

A magazine, *The Forerunner*, as the organ of the Work was set up and printed by hand in the Gardiner's home, and later in a room next to the blacksmith.

The village hall was built in which weekly concerts and plays were given. The culmination of the dramatic work was a Shakespearean pageant.

After two years of strenuous activity, Harold Large returned to London with the work so well organized, that the group was able to carry on.

The silent meeting grew in strength, and after his departure other friends were added, a simple form of ritual was used, and it was given the title of "The Society of the Southern Cross." From the beginning, definite guidance was received in rotation from three different sources, both Eastern and Western, the one that carried the group to the final stages of the quest being Western.

In 1910 the "Mission of Help" came to New Zealand, and Miss McLean arranged with Father Fitzgerald to meet members of the group at Bishop Court in Napier (a city close to Havelock North). The day before, one of the members at the silent meeting saw

Hebrew letters with which she was not familiar. Father Fitzgerald welcomed the group warmly and hearing of the "Quest" promised his assistance if we would work under his guidance. He produced a notebook in which were Hebrew letters. This visit filled the group with hope and expectation. They conducted their meeting according to the form he sent and kept in touch after his return to England. In due time he wrote that if further progress was to be made, people would have to come to England to teach. Within a week of receiving this letter, Reginald Gardiner through the generosity of John and Mason Chambers (nationally known architect), cabled 300 pounds to pay the passages. Advice followed that Dr. Felkin, with his wife and daughter would come for three months...

Though the wording leaves a lot to be desired, it does show the close knit aspect of the group on which Whare Ra was built. To some occult historians, some of these names will be known as members of other Stella Matutina Temples in England. Felkin wrote:

> It was about this time (Neville Meakin's admittance to a Sanatorium) that we received our first letter asking us if we would consider a trip to New Zealand, all expenses paid. At first it seemed an impossibility. My practice was purely a personal one; there was no one who could take charge during my absence and my

other work had grown steadily and demanded more of our time and attention. People had to be taught and helped and we could be ill spared. Yet on the other hand, it would be a terrible pity to let such an opportunity as this slip. We would be pioneers in a new world with virgin soil to work with.

Wynn Westscott, aided Felkin by giving him introductions to various Masonic groups in Australia (in Adelaide, Melbourne and Sydney). As a 32 degree Mason, Felkin was one of the highest to visit New Zealand. He was also appointed as an Inspector for the Societies of Rosicrucians in Anglia, which had a foothold in New Zealand at this stage, though he never officially took up this appointment.

During his three month stay in New Zealand, about a dozen members received the 5=6 grade, as all the training had to be telescoped into a short time period. The rituals were done in a large house in Havelock North. During this time, Mason Chambers and his wife donated some land on which rested the foundation of Whare Ra *(a Maori name meaning House of the Sun)*. The house itself was built by Chapman Taylor, with a huge vault in the basement and a temple area of between 1200 to 1500 square feet.

Before he left for England, Felkin consecrated the temple and left his daughter behind to further help those members with ritual and study work. At this time he wrote out a temple warrant for the foundation of the New Zealand order.

> The G.H. Chief Frater Aur Mem Mearab [Felkin] 8=3 and the V.H. Soror [Mrs. Felkin], members of the R.R. et A.C. under the Obedience of the Rites of Germany and Great Britain, and the V.H. Soror Maria Poimandres [Miss Felkin] 6=5 permit three Fraters
> Piscator Hominum 5=6
> Kiora 5=6
> Lux e Tenebris 5=6
> to form and rule both the Inner and Outer Order of the R.R. et A.C. and the Stella Matutina in Australia.
> For the Outer Order of the Smaragdum Thalasses Temple of the Stella Matutina in the Outer.
> Havelock North, Hawkes Bay, New Zealand

The Outer Order was the Smaragdum Thalasses, but it fell under the banner of the Stella Matutina in much the same way as the Guild of St. Raphael did in Britain. Felkin further wrote of this visit:

> That trip to New Zealand taught me more clearly than any other experience the necessity for action in cooperation with study. It puts teaching into dramatic form and welds together those who work together. There is a great deal more in it than that of course, but these two aspects were strongly impressed on me when I watched these handful of people taking part in what to them was an entirely strange form of work. There is a type of mind in which dramatic action is not merely uncongenial, but definitely repellent. But for those that can accept it, here is a beauty and impressiveness which they can find nowhere else.

The Enochian system never a high priority at Whare Ra, though according to Regardie, it was the crowning point of the Order teachings. Ritual instruction however was a par excellence as was Kabbalistic teachings. One individual, by the name of H. Campbell, did manage to study it fairly extensively and was the one who kept Enochian Chess alive. Campbell in his own right was quite a remarkable individual. He was the son of a wealthy grazier (rancher) who joined Whare Ra in its early days and fell under the patronage of Dr. Felkin. After Felkin's death in the late 1920s, Campbell went to England where he obtained a small apartment and went daily to the British Library to study the Dee manuscripts. He met many adepts in England of both the A.O. and S.M. Temples, and was the case Dion Fortune cited of the individual who had the bad experiences with the Abramelin system. His letter appeared in *The Occult Review* in 1927. With the help of Mrs. Felkin, he was able to rid himself of the negative influences of the squares.

On his return to New Zealand, Campbell brought back enlarged photos of all the Dee manuscripts. *[Author's note: I had the chance to see these some years ago, and was astounded at the amount of material, which would have cost hundreds of pounds to have done.]* With Mrs. Felkin's approval, he changed a number of the letters on the Enochian Tables from those of the H document which he deemed inaccurate. Campbell rose to the rank of 9=2, and on the death of Miss Felkin, he held the highest grade in the Order. This became something of an embarrassment, as the Triad of Chiefs were of the 8=3 level. In fact, Campbell had to initiate one of the Chiefs into the 9=2 level, as there were Adepti at Whare Ra who at 8=3, were equal to some of the Chiefs in rank.

At Whare Ra, there was a distinct search for astral masters which appeared to be in most of the old G.D. and S.M. temples. In the late 1930s, Mrs. Felkin started to receive astral messages concerning a master who was to come to New Zealand to teach. Some time later, she was put in touch with Australian anthroposophist Charles McDowell, who much to her surprise, received the same messages. In 1939, he came to New Zealand to meet Mrs. Felkin and to decide what they were going to do about the information received. It was decided to prepare a meeting place for this master to preach his gospel. The project was eventually called Tauhara, and has become a large international complex where those involved in esoteric studies can come and lecture.

Whare Ra underwent many of the trials and tribulations of the other temples, but with a membership exceeding three hundred, it was to be expected. The first major split in the Order came with Felkin's other Order, the O.T.R. (Order of the Round Table), an Arthurian Order in which Felkin was bestowed a knighthood by Neville Meakin. This was originally a small family Order. Its members were mainly made up of the elite of Whare Ra's Inner Order, and were to have shared Whare Ra equally with the R.R. et A.C. Elitism reared its ugly head and the O.T.R. opted for another base of operations, though its members still held footing in both camps. Things came to a head when Jack Taylor was appointed Chief of this Order after he walked out of Whare Ra in the late 1960s because of the non-Golden Dawn teachings being introduced into the R.R. et A.C. After what amounted to a showdown with the main Chief of Whare Ra over the leadership of the O.T.R., the group became firmly estranged from the original Temple. The head of the O.T.R. in England was Tudor Pole. (According to Taylor, Meakin's ancestral family name was Tudor.)

In 1964 a Bristol temple member, Charles Renn visited New Zealand. He was of the 6=5 rank in the Bristol Temple. After it closed, he came to New Zealand to take the 7=4 Grade from Whare Ra. In addition, Renn and his wife Beryl, held high rank in the Cromlech Temple or "Sun Order" as it was known in New Zealand. After obtaining the 7=4, he founded a "Temple of the Sun" in Havelock North. He had great expectations in the growth of the Cromlech Temple, but it only lasted a few short months. Jack Taylor and other Whare Ra members initially joined the Sun Temple to help him get started, but his colourful language and general disposition did not favour him with Whare Ra's elite. Renn died shortly after the Cromlech Temple closed.

Whare Ra had many trials and tribulations over teachings and personalities due to leadership issues. It became so bad that one of the Chiefs, Archie Shaw, actually walked out due to quarrels concerning teaching methods. This was a pity, as he was considered the most gifted of the Triad. The next major upheaval occurred with the introduction of Anne Davies of B.O.T.A. to New Zealand. Her visit to tiny New Zealand received the highest possible publicity which made many fantastic claims. Since many of the Whare Ra people had done, or were doing, the B.O.T.A. course, she was quite a celebrity. By this time, the Felkins had all died; many of those at Whare Ra felt a certain lack of direction of the Order. After a discussion between the major powers of Whare Ra, they agreed to have a major meeting at the Napier Hotel with Anne Davies. This meeting was to decide whether Whare Ra members would abandon the Golden Dawn teachings altogether for the direction of the B.O.T.A.

According to a former Chief, Anne Davies made a movie star entrance, but it was apparent to those with whom she spoke that giving up the Golden Dawn would mean adapting the Anne Davies style of leadership, which irked a lot of conservative New Zealanders. In Jack Taylor's own words:

> **During the meeting my wife got very worried, as it was clear to me and others that Anne Davies was claiming the adeptship of this entire planet. I then noticed one of the younger members [i.e. Ron Raison who became an OTR head] get up and rush outside. Since I thought he was ill, and at the insistence of my wife who thought that Anne Davies' persuasiveness might corrupt some of these younger people, I followed him out to his car where he was bent over all right, with laughter; he said he could not see Anne Davies' performance being topped by anyone.**

While some took this attitude, others did not, and one 5=6 member of Whare Ra was seconded by her to form a B.O.T.A. in New Zealand. The majority of the members of Whare Ra rejected her proposals, though for many it was touch and go for a while concerning the existence of the Temple. One of the problems Anne Davies faced was that she abhorred the Enochian Tablets, and any who came under the B.O.T.A. banner would have to cease working with them. Since Campbell's stature was high at Whare Ra, he strongly objected to this proposal as he had been using the Tablets for all of his adult life with no negative results. Later, after some Whare Ra members left to join the B.O.T.A., Anne Davies told some of the Whare Ra adepts that she would refuse to have anything to do with those who used the Tablets, in spite of the fact that the head of her New Zealand branch of the Order was a former 5=6 from Whare Ra. Apparently, her fear of the Enochian system was due to the fact that Michael Whitty, a former Golden Dawn Chief (of 7=4 rank) from the Thoth Hermes Temple in Chicago, came to an abrupt end which Paul Foster Case blamed on Enochiana. This prejudice had been passed on to Anne Davies.

The closure of Whare Ra left a lot of bitter feelings towards the Chiefs, as no meetings were held, and members were simply told that the temple had closed and that all papers had to be consigned to the flames. A huge truckload of Golden Dawn original, and later Temple documents, were so destroyed. The rest of the papers were burnt over a three day period, which gives some idea of the extent of destruction.

Just after the closure of Whare Ra, I made some inquiries through a family friend about the existence of a Golden Dawn Temple in the Havelock North area. After a letter exchange between ex-members which drew cryptic replies about the Order being finished and should be allowed to rest, I received a reply from Jack Taylor who took the opposite view to the negativity we had received from the other former members. He informed us that he had been told clairvoyantly that we were to expect to see him in the next few days, (Havelock North is some 400 miles from Wellington), and for us to come in to see him. What Jack could not have known is that we were booked to fly up to the Havelock North area the next day to visit relatives.

The following day we visited Jack and were met by a room full of Inner Order members from the Old Temple who chatted quite freely about the trials and tribulations of the Order. Since both my ex and I had been studying Order documents for some time, one could say that at the time we had the knowledge of the 5=6 Grade. We were appalled at the lack of information given out by those in charge during the final days of Whare Ra. Over the next few days, Jack Taylor decided that we would be initiated into the Order, and later into the R.R. et A.C. With the help and coaching of the many friends we met that first day, we founded the Thoth Hermes Temple a few years later, after Jack Taylor drafted up a charter for us to establish a temple in Wellington.

The closure of Whare Ra however did not stop the Golden Dawn System of Magic from being practiced among its ex-members. Those that had any real ability, in my opinion, still practiced together. One incident that Taylor recalled happened in 1984 when he was asked to help exorcise a building. Previously, objects had both moved and literally disappeared in front of people. One religious person who tried to exorcise the place was thrown bodily down the stairs by an unseen force.

When Taylor was asked to help, he gathered some of his former Whare Ra Inner Order colleagues and together they prepared for the exorcism. Though in his eighty-fifth year, and confined to a wheel chair, he was carried up the stairs and placed in the center of the room. With his magical sword and the Banner of the West around his neck, he proceeded with the exorcism which turned out to be successful. The master magician has struck again!

After corresponding with Regardie for a little over a year, he eventually visited the Thoth Hermes Temple in Wellington, New Zealand in August, 1983. During that visit, Regardie admitted to me that he was somewhat apprehensive about coming to New Zealand. He was not sure of the type of reception he would find due to his oath breaking in publishing the Golden Dawn years earlier. During the lifetime of Whare Ra, Regardie's name had been detested and his books banned. For those initiates, the prejudices of breaking the oath had been carried from one generation to the other. To them Regardie was a prime example of what not to do, though during his conversation with Jack Taylor, he was addressed as Frater Regardie; one of the Order's favored sons had returned to the fold.

Some years earlier Jack Taylor, who was a staunch stickler for the G.D. oath, told me that an oath was up to the dictates of one's conscience. In this respect, when my ex and I were put through the ceremonies, our oaths were reworded. At Thoth Hermes we were of the opinion that the important thing was not to restrict G.D. teaching to a few, but to try to foster its beliefs to all those who would listen. In both the Stella Matutina and the Golden Dawn Temples, there were more papers handed out in the Outer Order than the standard five Knowledge lectures, and these varied according to the knowledge and temperament of those in charge. Whare Ra was no exception, though these papers were hardly more than adequate with a bulk of the teachings being oral through personal tuition.

One of the major differences between the Whare Ra 5=6 course and that of the Thoth Hermes, was that in the latter, the four subgrades of the 5=6 were reintroduced. The Tarot and Talismanic study (not Consecration) were brought down to the Outer Order levels, as were the color scales. Regardie described the 5=6 papers of the Golden Dawn as, "A wealth of material with virtually no starting or finishing point which the Z.A.M. is swamped with, and it's sink or swim." At Thoth Hermes we came to the same conclusion. Enochiana is a prime example of this, and when one skryed the varying squares there was no given order to work from. Newer lectures were drawn up, where one worked through a series of progressive stages.

Since the early 1960s many of the Whare Ra Adepti had done or were still doing the BOTA course of Paul Foster Case. Some of the BOTA students counted as one of the last Order Chiefs among them Bethany Jones and Temple Chief Frank Salt along with Jack Taylor. The result was that there was cross pollination of ideas drifting into Whare Ra from BOTA–including some BOTA lectures. The BOTA concept of posting out four lessons a month for the next 16 years was something totally alien to the Whare Ra Adepti who had to do their own research almost on every subject. Some embraced it as an easier method of learning and some rejected it. On top of all this many at BOTA considered they were the original Golden Dawn, primarily at the behest of Will Chesterman, who eventually became world head of BOTA. Chesterman had once applied to join Whare Ra but was rejected, and it is something he never forgot. For many years afterward he had a love/hate relationship with Whare Ra.

The Order of the Table Round (OTR) and its association to Whare Ra has never really been fully discussed. This was an order that had equal status to the Stella Matutina and shared premises at Whare Ra. It was also the order that was dear to Felkin's heart and he was buried in its robes, and not that of the Chief Adept of Whare Ra. This was a family chivalric order that claimed Tudor heritage that was passed onto Felkin by Neville Meakin. Felkin then extended its boundaries to include like minded friends and associates and gradually into a more fraternal and also a more political unit. In its early years Felkin used it as an elitist order with the cream of Hawkes Bay society plus a governor general, premier and head of the armed forces to name but a few more prominent members. In order to make the order function alongside of Golden Dawn teachings, the leading lights of Whare Ra were also heads of the OTR. While the OTR drew many members in from Whare Ra (by invitation) it also drew heavily from various masonic groups which Felkin was influential in. The OTR was not a teaching group other than some brief explanations of the rituals. The idea was to go through the initiatic mystical experience of the images and some of the Arthurian myths and legends. It appears that Felkin wanted to keep a sharp divide between the two groups which eventually resulted in the OTR having its own hall after his death.

Miss Felkin was the last Chief Adept of Whare Ra to head both orders and on her death in 1962 the new head Chief of Whare Ra was John von Dadelzen who was not voted into the head position of the OTR and he lost out to Jack Taylor. This was the first time anything like that had happened and if there was rift between the two groups previously there was now a chasm, even though they shared similar membership.

John von Dadelzen was a lawyer and the son of a former Mayor of Havelock North and Inner Order member of Whare Ra. He married the daughter of a former Chief and those that trained under him and worked with him in ritual said that as far as the ritual mechanics went he was excellent, especially at where to stand and how to hold your sword and taught that things had to be done to the letter as well as being a good administrator. However it stopped there.

He was described to me by an Inner Order member of Whare Ra as a person who had memorised the lines for a role with absolutely no idea of what the role meant or the feeling behind it and appeared completely devoid of any emotional content in ritual, except putting on a happy face when he needed to. His pedigree for a Whare Ra Chief was impeccable but his inability to understand the inner dynamics of Golden Dawn ritual was soon becoming apparent as he assumed the mantle of primary Chief. He went through the grades almost effortlessly due to family influence but never remotely understood what they were about nor wanted to do the work required for the level he was at. When Miss Felkin (who was 9-2) died, von Dadelszen was 8=3 and had to get Hugh Campbell (who was never Chief due to a beverage issue) to initiate him into the 9=2 level. His stewardship lurched into another crises after losing the OTR vote, when his indecisiveness, domineering attitude and lack of insight caused one the Order Chiefs Archie Shaw (8=3), to resign from Whare Ra. At this point Jack Taylor was still a member of Whare Ra but von Dadelszen never forgave him for his loss of the OTR leadership to him and the ambivalent attitude shown towards Taylor when he made suggestive changes (some of which were the same category as what Archie Shaw had suggested) showed him the writing was on the wall for the end of Whare Ra. Just after 1965, Jack Taylor had had enough of von Dadelszen's stewardship and to make a point of it by simply not participating in Whare Ra rituals, as many had done, he formally resigned from the order, along with his wife (who was also 7=4) and concentrated on the OTR, which in many respects he redefined.

John von Dadlezen

How von Dadelszen handled the drop in membership was that he simply ignored it and concentrated his energies to Mrs. Felkin's pet project of establishing a teaching and learning centre at a place called Tahaura on the shores of Lake Taupo. This was the third branch of the tree after Whare Ra and the OTR and the histories of all three branches are so interwoven it is difficult to separate them.

The Tauhara trust was formed in 1938 with sixty acres of land, was consecrated and set aside. To a certain extent it stagnated due to the war years with the original site being sold off to pay for rising rates and the remainder taken by the local council. A new site was needed. The project staggered on until the sale of Whare Ra in 1978 with the finance going into the Tauhara trust's coffers with the Whare Ra's last three Order Chiefs, John von Dadelszen, Nancy Hobson and Bethany Jones being the three trustees of Tauhara. Bethany Jones informed a mentor of ours, Babara Nairn, that she felt the two other Chiefs had bullied her into winding up the temple and felt overwhelmed and eventually gave into their demands. Tauhara was very much suited to von Dadelszen's temperament as he could officiate, be a leading light at social gatherings and take little responsibility and could relieve himself of the burden of Whare Ra with its heavy emphasis on traditions.

While my own story has been discussed with Jack Taylor, there is another story that should be told regarding former Hierophant and Temple Chief Frank Salt. Like

Jack Taylor, Frank also took membership in BOTA and started their course. During this time Frank made contact with Dr. Tony Fuller, who at that stage was a high ranking member of BOTA and whose responsibilities in that order had him frequently travelling the country making contacts with BOTA members. Tony had a strong interest in the history of Whare Ra and knew many of the people that had instructed me in the Golden Dawn tradition plus he had the added advantage of one set of Whare Ra papers up to the 7=4 which he had inherited through an in-law. Frank Salt was then based in a masonic retirement home had taken the odd student who had shown interest but to the best of my knowledge had initiated only one person into the Inner Order level, who is known in the outer world as Kasmillos–before Tony. By the time Tony studied under Frank he was at the top level of BOTA and a long time ritualist, plus his own Golden Dawn studies which had taken him well past the 5=6 level. Frank decided to take Tony as a student, on the Whare Ra advanced levels which culminated in Frank Salt contacting former Chief Archie Shaw and the both of them initiating him into the 7=4 level in a vault which Archie had built after leaving Whare Ra.

I had known Frank Salt for a number of years and had regular correspondence and phone calls. If Jack did not know what I was after I would often write or phone Frank. Frank had a very old fashioned approach and made you dig for every morsel of information often in a very convoluted manner and the opposite of Jack Taylor (another Gemini like myself) and you had to try and keep up with him. I can appreciate what Tony and Kasmillos went through. Apart from Tony's initiation into the higher levels of Whare Ra, he also was taken through all the levels of the Sun Order (Cromlech Temple) and is well versed in understanding the crossover between the Cromlech Temple philosophy and what was adopted by the AO temples. Now based in England, Tony has possibly the best Golden Dawn collection of Golden Dawn documents in the world today and has been influential in promulgating a number of Golden Dawn temples and is currently writing a book on Whare Ra history and is still active in Golden Dawn research. Kasmillos is still active in Golden Dawn temple work and prefers anonymity.

CHAPTER 2

THE ORIGINS OF THE ROSICRUCIAN ORDER

The initial impetus of the Golden Dawn's Inner Order, the Rosae Rubea et Aurea Crucis (The Red Rose and the Cross of Gold), stemmed from Rosicrucian sources which made the cornerstone of their teachings the first two Rosicrucian manifestos published in the 17th century by an anonymous authorship. Within the Golden Dawn's Inner Order, elaborate rituals were used, utilizing props and settings that described the finding of the vault of Christian Rosenkruetz and the teachings he had to offer humanity. The basis for these were contained in both the "Fama" and "Confessio" manifestoes. In the Adeptus Minor Ritual of the 5=6 Grade the following summation of these two documents is read to the Postulant.

"In 1378 the Chief and Originator of our Fraternity was born in Europe. He was the son of noble but poor parents, and was placed in a cloister at the age of five where he learned some Greek and Latin. While yet a youth, he accompanied a certain Brother P.A.L. on a pilgrimage to the Holy Land; but the latter, dying at Cyprus, he himself went to Damascus. There was then in Arabia a Temple of the Order which was called in the Hebrew tongue 'Damkar': that is, 'The Blood of the Lamb.' There he was duly initiated, and took the Mystic title Christian Rosenkreutz, or Christian of the Rose Cross. He then so improved his knowledge of the Arabian tongue, that in the following year he translated the book 'M' into Latin, which he afterwards brought back with him to Europe.

"After three years he went into Egypt, where there was another Temple of the Order. There he remained for a time still studying the mysteries of Nature. After this, he travelled by sea to the city of Fessa, where he was welcomed at the Temple established there. While at the Temple, he obtained the knowledge and acquaintance of the habitants of the Elements, who revealed unto him many of their secrets. Of the Fraternity, he confessed that they had not retained their Wisdom in its Primal purity, and that their Kabala was to a certain extent altered to their religion. Nevertheless, he learned much there. After a stay of two years he came to Spain, where he endeavoured to reform the errors of the learned according to the pure knowledge he had received. But this was to them a laughing matter, and they reviled and rejected him, even as the prophets of old were rejected. Thus also was he treated by those of his own and other nations when he showed them the errors that had crept into their religions. So, after five years residence in Germany, he initiated three of his former monastic brethren, Fraters G.W., I.A., and I.O., who had more knowledge than many others at the time. And by these four was made the foundation of the Fraternity in Europe.

These three worked and studied at the writings and other knowledge which C.R.C. had brought with him, and by them was some of the Magical Language transcribed (which was that of the Elemental Tablets) and a dictionary thereof made; and the Rituals and part of the Book 'M' were transcribed.

"For the True Order of the Rose Cross descendeth into the heights—even unto the Throne of God Himself, and includeth even Archangels, Angels and Spirits.

"These four Fraters also erected a building to serve as a Temple and Headquarters of their Order, and called it Collegium and Spiritum Sanctum, or the College of the Holy Spirit. This now being finished, and the work of establishing the Order began extremely heavy; and because they devoted much time to the healing of the sick and possessed who resorted to them, they initiated four others, viz: Fraters R.C. (the son of the deceased father's brother of C.R.C.), C.B. a skillful artist, and P.D., who was to be Cancellarius; all being Germans except I.A., and now eight in number. Their agreement was:

    1. That none of them should profess any other thing, but cure sick, and that freely.
    2. That they should not be constrained to wear any distinctive dress, but therein follow the custom of the country.
    3. That every year on the day of Corpus Christi, they should meet at the Collegium and Spiritum Sanctum, or write the cause of absence.
    4. Every one should look for some worthy person of either sex, who after his decease might succeed him.
    5. The word R.C. was to be their mark, seal, and character. The Fraternity was to remain secret for one hundred years. Five of the Fraters were to travel in different countries, and two were to remain with Christian Rosenkreutz.

"Frater I.O. was the first to die, and then in England, where he had wrought many wonderful cures. He was an expert Kabbalist, as his book '*H*' witnesseth. His death had been previously foretold him by C.R.C. But those who were later admitted were of the First Order, and knew not when C.R. died; and save what they learned from Frater A., the successor of D. of the second Order, and from their library after his death, knew little of the earlier and higher Members, and of the Founder, nor yet whether those of the Second Order were admitted to the Wisdom of the highest members. The discovery then of the tomb wherein that highly illuminated Man of God, our Father C.R.C. was buried occurred as follows.

"After Frater A. died in Gallia Narbonensi, there succeeded in his place Frater N.N. He, while repairing a part of the building of the College of the Holy Spirit, endeavoured to remove a brass memorial tablet which bore the names of certain brethren, and some other things. In this tablet was the head of a strong nail or bolt, such that when the tablet was forcibly wrenched away, it pulled with it a large stone which partially uncovered a secret door, upon which was inscribed in large letters 'Post CXX Annos Patebo' — "After a hundred and twenty years I shall open,' with the year of our Lord under, 1484. Frater N.N., and those with him then cleared away the rest of the brickwork, but let it remain that night unopened as they wished first to consult the R.O.T.A.

"On the following morning, Frater N.N. and his companions forced open the door, and there appeared to their sight a Tomb of Seven Sides and Seven Corners. Every side was five feet broad, and eight feet high. Although in the Tomb of the Sun does not shine, it is lit by the symbolic Rose of our Order in the centre of the first heptagonal ceiling. In the midst of the Tomb stands a circular altar, and after having raised the brazen plate or lid of the Pastos, discover the body of our Founder, with all the ornaments and insignia...Upon his breast was the Book 'T,' a scroll explaining in full the mystic Tarot; at the end of which was written a brief paragraph concerning Christian Rosenkreutz, beneath which earlier Fraters had inscribed their names. Following this came the names of the three Highest Chiefs of the Order, viz:

Frater Hugo Alverda, the Phrisian, in the 576th year of this age.

Frater Francisco de Bry, the Gaul, in the 495th year of this age.

Frater Elman Zata, the Arab, in the 463rd year of his age.

Last of all was written: Ex Deo Mascimur; in Yesheshuah Morimur; Per Spiritum Sanctum Reviviscimus. 'In God are we born, in Yeheshuah we die, through the Holy Spirit we rise again.' So then, our Frater N.N. and his companions reclosed the Pastos for a time, set the Altar over it, shut the Door of the Tomb, and placed their seals upon it."

Though slightly slanted from the Order's perspective, it does give an indication of the content of the Rosicrucian documents and their teachings. The official history of the Order, written by Wynn Wescott (under the initials of his Order motto) further provides us with a bridge in which to interpret the Rosicrucian history relating directly to the R.R. et A.C.:

History of the Rosicrucian Order
by G.H. Frater N.O.M.

The opening words of that part of the 5=6 Ritual which deals with the History of the Order of the R.C. are as follows:

> **Know them O Aspirant, that the Order of the Rose and Cross hath existed from time immemorial and that its mystic rites were practiced and its hidden knowledge communicated in the initiations of the various races of Antiquity: Egypt, Eleusis, Samothrace, Persia, Chaldea, and India alike cherished these mysteries, and thus handed down to posterity the Secret Wisdom of the Ancient Ages...**

This statement is one which comes home to every member of the 5=6 Grade, for although one in that position is but on the threshold of genuinely serious Occult study and development, it is easy enough to trace the masterful manner in which our mystic knowledge has been consolidated; and the essential unity of the system speaks eloquently of the Wisdom which formulated it.

Albeit, the manner of its introduction into medieval Europe is chiefly interesting to us. C.R. is the great figure-head around which has clustered the most romantic traditions of medieval Occultism. History has not passed down the real name of this unique character: for C.R. is obviously a fictitious or assumed name chosen for mystic purposes.

Born in 1378 and dying in 1484, a life of 106 years was apparently the term of his physical manifestation: and to his exertions and efforts, it is that we may describe the great reformation of Occultism in the West. Fired by a noble purpose and ensouled by divine energies, his was the ideal of a life of Occult usefulness: it reckons little if the world knew nought of that obscure personality, but it was a matter of supreme importance to the progress of Western Occultism; and the full significance of this observation will probably be only appreciated by you in proportion as you may advance hereafter. The first years of his eventful life were spent in study: both intellectual and occult, to be eventually followed by a series of initiations at several places (outside of Europe) where there existed Temples of our Order. "Thus were laid foundations thereon to erect a more extended superstructure of practical application," and, having chosen three other Fraters to share with him the heat and burden of the day, the establishment of the Order was effected in Europe. With the principal features of their subsequent activity you are already familiar, and it suffices to say that when our Founder "entered unto his chamber" his work was accomplished, and every member among us hereby placed under a lasting debt of gratitude.

It is to be observed that there are three important epochs in the history of the Rosicrucian Order: the first being the life period of Christian Rosycross, who died before the time of the Protestant reformation; the second, the 120 years of silence and secrecy, being the period 1484 to 1604; and the third period subsequent to and since the Reformation. It was during this last period that the opening of the Vault formed the historical basis for the subsequent publication of the *"Fama Fraternitatis"*; or "A Discovery of the Most Laudable Order of the Rosy Cross," the publication of which took place at Cassel in 1614, though this tract is dated 1610. This event called forth the most intense curiosity and excitement. The enormous effect which it had upon the learned world of the time may be better understood when it is stated that there were no fewer than 600 tracts at Berlin, all criticizing— either favourably or otherwise—the mysterious association revealed by the *"Fama."* In 1614, then, pubic attention was directed to the Order for the first time and many thousands are said to have responded to the invitation offered by the "*Fama*": those who were admitted were bound over to keep the matter a secret, and the larger proportion who received no response to their overtures believed the whole thing an illusion.

It will be obvious upon reflection, that the ceremonies and allotment of rituals and instructions of the Second Order as now existing cannot be identical with that which was obtained prior to the opening of the Vault, because the principal symbolism of the 5=6 and 7=4 respectively: the former, a degree of death and solemnity referring to the precedent stage of obscuration, during which silent study and meditation may be considered as the typical condition. The latter, the Grade of Adeptus Exemptus, being referred to the higher and more exalted rank and attainments of he who founded the Rosicrucian Order as a new formulation of the occult philosophy or Wisdom religion which, we cannot doubt, has never been entirely absent since the manifestation of the human intellect with a capacity for the apprehension of things Divine.

On comparing the esoteric historical account given in the *Fama* with that contained in our 5=6 Ritual, several important divergencies and discrepancies become apparent. The *Fama* was written for the public, and is therefore not absolutely correct. Instances of the 'blinds' introduced into the *Fama* occur where, in the description of the Vault, it is stated "This is all clear and bright, as also the seventh (the Seven Sides—the 7th was not different) side and the two heptagons..." And again, later on: "Every Side or Wall is parted into ten squares, every one with their several figures and sentences..." "Every side or Wall" is moreover represented as having a door for a chest wherein many things and books lay, including the vocabularium of Paracelsus who lived from 1493 to 1541, or during the 120 years of closure previously referred to. This was an obvious inconsistency, and was in fact an intentional blind inserted for the purpose of disappointing the critics of that day. (The critic is rarely or never an Occultist. To ensure the exclusion of such men, the Society cunningly authorized the publication of a tract, with an intentional blot in it which would condemn it immediately in their eyes and so kept such men from clamouring for admission.) For be it remembered, the *Fama* was an official manifesto; the publication of which was authorized by the Fraters then empowered. Subsequently, on account of the great stir roused by its publication, and especially on the assertion that the principles of the Order were subversive to the simple orthodox faith of Christianity, its publication by Valentine Andreas was authorized (in 1615) with a Supplement under the title of *"Confession Fraternitatis R.C. ad Erudotos Europa."* This was prefaced by an advertisement to the effect that the "gentle reader should find incorporated in our Confession 37 reasons of our purpose and intention, the which according to thy pleasure mayest seek out and compare together, considering within thyself if they be sufficient to allure thee." The point of this, however, is that examination of the contents does not reveal the 37 reasons, nor do the Hebrew Letters representing that number form any Word which might seem to be the secret meaning, but by Temurah, two pregnant words are shown forth: thus LHB=30+5+2=Flame, Lux, Light. Illumination and LGD=20+3+4="For the Society," or army.

There is another reference to Paracelsus in the *Fama* which is of curious interest. It runs: "although he was not of our fraternity, yet nevertheless hath he dignity read over

Book *M.*, whereby his sharp ingenium was exalted." Now Paracelsus was taught by Johann Trithemius of Spanheim, Abbot of Wurtzburg, and Solomon Trismosin. He also travelled in the East, and being taken captive in Tarty, (compare with H.P.B.'s initiation in Tibet. Paracelsus was not a Rosicrucian, yet after initiation taught very similar tenets. He also found another allied Temple in the East), was initiated there. Moreover, he is said to have received the Stone in Constantinople, from one Sigismund Fugger.

Although the *Fama* is in some cases deficient in its historical account, it contains here and there redundant descriptions, which affords food for reflection. Thus, it is said, "In another chest were looking glasses of diverse virtues, as also in other places were little bells, burning lamps, and chiefly wonderful artificial songs...." The latter referring of course to the Mantrams of the easterns: Carmina or incantations, being instructions on the vibratory mode of pronouncing divine names.

The only other important Rosicrucian publication was a very curious work entitled the *Hermetic Romance, or the Chymical Wedding*, which likewise excited much controversy. It is full of perplexities (for the casual reader), though the meaning is entirely allegorical and only to be seized by violence. Of this class of study, all that can be said is "Sometimes a light surprises the student on his way." The date of publication was 1616, the year following the appearance of the *Confesso Frateritatis*.

I should mention that an English translation of the *Fama* was done in London by Eugenius Philalthes, in 1652. At that time he was Supreme Magas in Anglia, or Chief Adept in charge of our phraseology.

In conclusion, it only remains for me to point out that while the historical element has a unique interest for every member of the 5=6 Grade of the Second Order, this in itself is a minor consideration as compared with the mystic symbolism involved therein. The 120 years has other references, as the 5=6 Ritual itself testifies. This was the number of Princes, which Darius set over his Kingdom; that Daniel was a Magus among the Chaldees, while another hint as to its meaning lies in the suggestion as to how that number was arrived at.

In the 5=6 Grade, the symbolism of the Rainbow Colours is especially exemplified: a range of Colour which may be said to be the most apparent and obvious, while the 6=5 Grade is of interest to many of us, especially because the colouring is different. The 7=4 Grade refers still further back and possesses an even more arcane symbolism..."

The above paper by Wescott clearly shows that the Golden Dawn and it Inner Order the R.R. et A.C. hinges on interpretations. The first is that series of Cyphers (based on an alchemical treatise and published in the Polygraphiae of Johann Trithmius), was found in a book stall; while the second says that these papers found their way into Wescott's hands through the papers Fred Hockley (1808-85), a prominent Mason, Rosicrucian and Spiritualist. At any rate once Wescott had the papers, he asked Mathers to translate and expand them into workable Grade Rituals. It is said that with these Cyphers was an address of a certain S.D.A. in Germany to whom Wynn Wescott wrote, and in return received a Charter promoting him and two others (Mathers and Woodman) to the rank of 5=6 Grade. These original Cyphers when translated are skeletonic, and a comparison to the full blown rituals of the Golden Dawn (as published in the Complete G.D.) is extremely interesting, for these are the cornerstone upon which the Golden Dawn was built.

THE CYPHER MANUSCRIPTS

NOUGHT = NOUGHT
OPENING

All assemble and put on Sashes, Collars, Lamens

H.	I. Fratres and Sorores of this Temple of the Golden Dawn assist me to open in the Grade of Neophyte.
K.	Hekas. Hekas. Este. Bebeloi.
H.	See to guarding and who is present.
H.	Who are the Officers?
HS.	They are H. HS. and HG. Principal.
H.	They have these in common?
HS.	The Letter H emblem of Breath and Life.
H.	What other Officers?
HS.	Stolistes Dadouchos and Kerux and a Sentinel who is outside and armed.

DAD. I am in the South with Censer and am Heat.

STOL. I am in North with Water and am Cold and Moisture.

K. I am inside Door. I arrange Hall. I carry Lamp, announce Report, and lead all Circumambulations.

HG. I am between Pillars and preside over Symbolic Gate of Occultism. I reconcile Light and Darkness. My White Robe is Purity. I carry a Mitre Headed Sceptre=Religion to Guide and Regulate Life and Guide higher aspirations of Soul.

HS. I am in West. I am Darkness. My Robe is Black. I carry a Sword=Judgement. My banner Twilight. I am Fortitude.

H. I am on Throne of East=Rising Sun. I rule and govern Hall and members of all Grades. My Robe is Red. I hold Sceptre and Banner of East. I expound Mysteries. I am Power Light Mercy and Wisdom.

H. Fra Stol purify with ▽

H. Frad Dad purify with △

H. Let us Circumambulate in Light.

H. It is accomplished. Let us adore.

H. Holy art Thou Lord of the Universe whom Nature has not formed the Vast and the Mighty One Lord of Light and Darkness.

H.	Frater K. proclaim Temple open.
K.	I proclaim Sun has arisen.
H.	Khabs
HS.	AM
HG.	Pekht
HS.	Konx
HG.	OM
H.	Pax
HG.	Light
H.	In
HS.	Extension

CLOSE

H.	I. (Knocks once) Hekas Hekas Este Bebeloi
H.	Soreres Fratresque assist to close Temple.
HS.	I.
K.	(Sees Hall guarded)
HS.	(Sees none but Neophyte is present.)
STOL.	(Purifies with ▽)
DAD.	(Purifies with △) (E.S.W. and N.)

H.	(Circumambulate reverse. Not the H–K HG HS ST DAD)
H.	Let us adore Lord of Universe. Let us take the Mystic repast of ר(4) elements △ △ ▽ ▽ (should be ▽) Rose=△ -Silence.
K.	(Last finishes Wine) It is Finished.
H.	Tetelestai.
H.	May this assist us in search for Quintessence– Summum Bonum. Wisdom Happiness.
H.	Khabs
HS.	AM
HG.	Pekht.
HS.	Knox
HG.	OM
H.	Pax
HG.	Light
H.	In
HS.	Extension

0=0 NOUGHT=NOUGHT
ADMISSION

H.	By dispensation I order H.G. to prepare the Candidate. (Blinds her or him. ג (3) Ropes.)

THE SECRET INNER ORDER RITUALS OF THE GOLDEN DAWN

H. (Admit. loses Name. Takes Motto.)

K. Refuses admission until censed and cross marked by DAD and STOL. Candidate asking for Light is taken to Altar and forces to take an Obligation to Secrecy under threats of expulsion and death or palsy from hostile current of will. Candidate put in North. H. Tells her or him to pass from Dark to Light. Circumambulate in Darkness.

K. (Leading with Red Lamp. Candidate stopped in N.E. until purified and consecrated.)

HG. (Leads Candidate to West.)

HS. Pass not until you know my Name.

C. Darkness.

HS. Fear not. Pass on.

C. (Stopped in N.E. STOL and DAD. Again.)

H. Pass not til you know my Name.

C. Light Dawning art Thou.

H. Avoid that which is unbalanced. Kneel and Pray.

H HS HG & Candidate stand around Altar. Emblems on High. Light restored.

KHABS – AM – PEKHT
KONX – OM – PAX
LIGHT – IN – EXTENSION

K steps up H shows K and Lamp to C as Hidden Light of Occult Science.

H. Let HS. give signs of a Neophyte.

H.S. (Step = one short step by left foot. Saluting Sign= both hands out front. Silent Sign = left forefinger on lip. Token=seize fingers only at second time.)

HAR PAR KRAT

HS. (Also gives a changeable Password in use for (6) months.)

HS. (Places her or him between Pillars.)

H. Let final Consecration be done.

HG. (Invests with ▷)

H. (Congratulates)

H. (Explains Hoodwink–and Cord–Altar a Double Cube=Black. White ▲ and Red+ on it. ▲ △ ▽ ▽ also on Atar–Two Pillars of Hermes–Seth–Solomon=Eternal Equilibrium.

(9)

H. (Active and Passive. Severity and Mercy. Fixed and Volatile. A Lamp on Each. Pillars have Egyptian figures on them. Between them is the Path of Occult Science. Note △ and Riam of Life.)

HS.	Throne Robe Sword.
HG.	(Between Pillars White Mitre Sceptre. He is Reconciler.)
K.	(With his Wand and Lamp. STOL + Cup=Cold. DAD+Censer=Heat.)
K.	(Proclaims new Neophyte.)
HS.	(Addresses Neophyte and exhorts to memory to honour God as our Light.) Never condemn others' Religion. Be Secret. Study Equilibrium. Each unbalance is Evil. Persevere.
H.	(Tells subjects of necessary study. ד (4) elements Zodiac Signs Planets Houses Exhaltation– Triplicities–Letters and Numbers in Hebrew– the Ten Sephiroth.)
H.	(No advance except by permit of Second Order.

(1=10) ZELATOR
ADMISSION

H.	(Announces permission to advance the Neophyte.)
HG.	(Prepares Neophyte.)

(Neophyte is blinded. Carries Knocks III III I I I)

NEO.	Let me enter.
K.	I will.

H.	(Psalm קבוא. (127-1) By what aid seek entry.
NEO.	By אדני (Adonai)–Knowledge–Permission. Secrets of 0 0 –By 卍
H.	(Gives Signs–Words.)
H.	(Pledges Neophyte.)
NEO.	I Pledge. Kneels. Swears by ▽ (Earth).
H.	(Remove blind–Throw Salt. NEO rises. ST DAD Purify.)
H.	(Congratulates on progress.)
H.	(Reads Genesis ב.חטי (2-8, 9, 10). Gives Allegory of תוכלם (Malkuth) Two Paths. סנרלפון למש מטטכון (Metatron–Samuel–Sandalphon.)
H.	(Describes Paths Three תשכ from תוכלם to Higher Sephiroth.)
H.	(Explains picture of Flaming Sword.)
H.	(Altar has Red+ of Kerubim inside △ .)
H.	Is the ▽ Grade shews ▽ Tables as in old MSS.)

H.	(卍 is יז (17) squares out of כה squares. These are ☉ △ △▽ ▽ and Zodiac.)
H.	Quits Temple.

(Neophyte reenters by Knocks III II I I I)

H.	(Addresses Neophyte. DAD censes)
H.	Before you is the Laver of Brass. It means Waters of Creation.
H.	Klippoth Below–Souls Above.

Neophyte enters Path of Evil.

HIER.	(Stops Neophyte who claims by אדני (Adonai) as Samuel speaks as Darkness and Evil– Neophyte retires.)
NEO.	(Advances to Heg.)
HEG.	(Stops NEO. As מטטרון (Metatron) stops NEO. Because too Bright.)
NEO.	(Retires.)
NEO.	(Goes up Middle.)
H.	(As Sandalphon with Sign of א = י (1=10) Checks HI. and HEG.)
H.	I am Reconciler–I am Left KRUB as HEG is Right KRUB and Male.

H.	Genesis ב.כ.ה
H.	(Confers secrets.)
H.	(Step Left then Right. Beyond is Sign as Grasp hands thumbs make over מלכה ה אדני (Adonai h'Melekh) Pass= כה) 
H.	(Gives Sash.)
STOL.	(Marks ✝)
NEO.	(Enters Holy Place)
HI.	(Stops NEO. who signs as NEO.)
HEG.	(Leads NEO. to North and explains

Picture of [pentagram surrounded by 12 circles] יב (12) Circles Lamp

which are the Zodiac Signs and Tribes and the יב(12) changes of the Name יהוה (IHVH) tells of יב.ז.ג. (3, 7, 12) sets of Hebrew Letters. The ד (4) elements which are Lion–Man–Bull–Eagle ☆ = ה the Whole Rose of Creation.

Hierus–takes NEO. to South. Shows ↑ (7) pointed Star Lamp= ↑ (7) Branched Candlestick=Heptagram= ↑ (7) Planets–Palaces of Assiah=Material World= (7) Churches a △ in each of ↑ (7) Circles with Names △ =Creation–Days of Week– ↑ (7) Stars.

Hierophant takes Neophyte to Altar. Censes It. This is the Altar of Incense. Double Cube= י (10) Squares. Base מלכות (Malkuth)=only One Seen God is behind Altar. I lack not Gold on Altar were ג (3) things △.▽. Incense

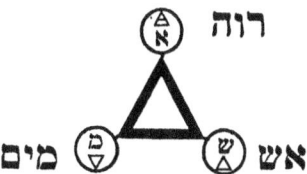

I name you Pereclinus De Faustis or Zelathor=Zelator

K.   (Proclaims)

H.   (Explains מרעא - עשר - אער - מלכות = Gate=אדני in Full Path (10) Resplendent Intelligence sits in בינה (Binah)= רהר of מארת gives Influx to Metatron.)

H.   (Declares יה (15) necessary studies ג (3) Principles–Metals–Alchemia   King Queen יב (12 Houses–Aspects Querent– ד (4) Classes Astrology–Tree of Life ג (3) Pillars–Elementals–Kerubim–Laver. Altar Klippoth– י (10) Heavens Assiah ד (4) Worlds– כב (22) Tarot Trumps.)

CLOSING

H.   (Zelators assist closing.)

K.   (Sees and Guards.)

H.	(Let us adore the Lord and King of אדני הא ארץ (Adonai ha Aretz, Adonai Melekh). אדני מלכה
H.	(Recites Prayer of the Gnomes.)
H.	(Depart in Peace.)
H.	(In the Name of אדני (Adonai) I close this Temple of Zelators.)
H.	(III III I I I)
HI.	(III III I I I)
HE.	(III III I I I)

א (1) TO ב (2) KNOWLEDGE
(4) WORLDS OF THE QABBALISTS ARE:

אצילות (ALZILUTH)=Pure Deity
בריאה (BRIAH)=Creative–Archangelic
יצירה (YETZIRAH)=Angels
עשיה (ASSIAH)=Shells Man Demons

TAROT SUITS

Wands or Batons=Diamonds/Cups=Hearts/Swords=Spades/Pentacles or Coins=Clubs. Of these there are י (10)

FOR THIS PURPOSE ALSO

♒	Matthew	▽	Man
♌	Mark	△	Lion
♉	Luke	▽̄	Earth
♏	John	△	Air

ד (4) SORTS OF ELEMENTALS ARE
Gnomes=▽̄ Undines=▽ Sylphs=△ Salamanders=△

ב = ט (2=9) THEORICUS

Officers H. HS. HG. KX.

Opening arrange as far בך (32) Path

H.	(Calls to order–Sees Guarding–Who Present. Signs Given).
HG.	(ב Grade= △ (Air))
HS.	(ב Grade=Luna)
HG.	(Its Path בך (32)= ת)
H.	(Prayer to שדי אלהי (Shaddai Al Chai))

All Pass to East.

H makes

                ACTIVES   PASSIVES   FOR   (AIR)

H.	Let Sylphs Adore יהוה (IHVH) and שדי אלהי (SHADDAI AL CHAI
H.	(Signs ♒ (sic) Man–Raphael)
H.	(With ✝ in Names of ORO IBAH AOZPI in Great East Tablet and BATAIVAH.)

All go to places

H.	(Declares open III III III)
HS.	(III III III)
HG.	(III III III)

CLOSE

H.   (Calls to Order–Guard–who presents)

H.   Prayer Adore Lord of △ all to East.

H.   (Prayer of Sylphs as in old MSS.)

H.

(Dismisses Sylphs in Name of שדי אלהי SHADDAI AL CHAI)

H.   (III III III)

HS. (III III III)

HG. (III III III)

ADMISSION PATH לב

H.   (Calls to Order)

HG. (Blinds Zelator who bears )

H.   (Has ⟁)

HS. (Has ♀)

HG. (Has   )

KX. (Has ⊖ Salt.)

Zelator admitted and put in East. Gives Sign obligated.
Lights restored to Zelator but Temple is Dark.
Zelator swears by Sylphs.

H.   (Shows Portals תשק only Open.)

K. (As Anubis Guides.)

Zelator goes with ✝ and Banner of East round Hall. SL–Sphynx said I am ♒ Man the Synthesis.

H. (Stops Z. with Mask of Osiris).

K. & Z. (Thou art Air and Sun. I come with א (Air)

H. (Signs ♒ as Man.)

HS. I as Osiris.

HG. (with Mask of Lion stops Z.)

H. & Z. Thou art Leo. I come with 🜂 (Fire)

HI. (Signs ♌)

HS. I passed through Gates of Heaven Oh Lord of Truth.

HI. (Stops Z. with ▽ saying) I as Mask of Eagle stop you. Mistress of △ and a Sun are you.

Z. I come as ♏ (Water)

HS. (Signs ♏ pass on.)

HS. (O Lord of Light. Darkness fleeth.)

K. (Stops Z. as Priest with Mask of ♉ in North.)

HG. & Z. Bull of Earth are you and Sun as Night. We come with שמא Banner and ✝ .

K. (Signs ♉ pass on.)

H.	(Describes ⟨glyph⟩ of בכ (22) Squares and ת Path and לא (31) Key of Tarot which עב (72) Circles Round. Queen Isis=Sandalphon.) Bears Wands. Has Crossed. He is ז (7) Pointed Star ד (4) Kerubim at Corners.)
HG.	(Takes Z. Shews Eden–a Circle with ז (7) Squares ד (4) Rivers and Tree inside.)
K.	(Shews Gehenna ז (7) Infernals and ז (7) Seas.)
H.	(Confers Name of Lord of לב (32nd) Path.)

Zelator readmitted with HG. by III III III.

H.	(Gives summary of earlier Grades. S.S. and Ark and Kerubim.)
Z.	(Put in West)
Z.	(Presents ⟨glyph⟩)
HS.	(Explains it by a Picture.)
H.	(Shows Altar with Tree of Life. Serpentine Figure and Letters on the Paths. (2)= ב (9)= ת = סיוד (YESOD) The Path of ת. Sign=Atlas ⟨glyph⟩ Word= שדי אלהי SHADDAI EL CHAI) and pass נה (55) ת Path explains Badge. 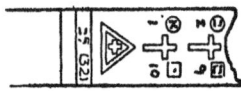

	The Right Portal goes to ד = ז (4=7)
	The Left Portal goes to ג = ח (3=8)
	The Central goes to Higher.)
H.	(Shows Tablet of Air △ and Kamea of Luna. ☽ Note also Hod Elim Chashmudai shows ☽ on Tree of Life.)
HS.	(Shows Alchemic Sephiroth. Two forms of אשמצרפ)
HG.	(Shows Lineal Figures and Plants)
K.	(Shows Figures of Geomancy)
H.	You are now Poraios De Rejectis.
K.	(Proclaims Her or Him)
H.	(Describes subjects for ג = ח (3=8))

ג (3)= ח (8) – H. HS. HG. PRACTICUS
OPENING

H.	(Sees to Guarding.)
H.	(Sees who is present–Signs given.)
HG.	(to ▽)
HS.	(to ☿)
HG.	(Paths are א ל (31) and ל (30) of ש and ר Reflection of Sphere of △ (Fire) ר Reflection of (Sun))

H. Let us Adore King of אלהים צבאות
(ELOHIM TZABOATH)
(Open in the Names of
(AL, ELOHIM TZABOATH) אל אלהים צבאות
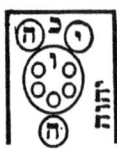 GABRIEL †
EMPEH ARSEL GIAOL
RA AGIOSEL
which are the Names found in The Great Western Quadrangle of)

H. HS. HG. (I III I III.)

FOR PATH לב (31) TABLETS OF –KEY   (20) OF TAROT

 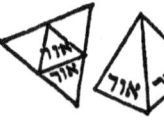

HEAVENS   AVERSE!   PYRAMID TO ADMIT
Path לב (31)

H. (Take △ and follow Axiokersa the Kabir)

H. (As Axieros speaks in the Oracles of Zoroaster on Ideas and Intellectuals.)

H. (Continues as Axiokersos.) I am the Left Basal Angle of △ Flame.

HG. I am the Right Basal Angle Astral and Fluid Fire.

H. (Speaks) Stoop Not—Nature persuades STROPHALOS / MNIZOURIN / Change not Names / Voice of Fire.

THE SECRET INNER ORDER RITUALS OF THE GOLDEN DAWN

H.   (Explains ⟁ and נפ (31) Path=Perpetual Intelligence.)

H.   (Shows and explains Key ב (20) Which is much more than the Last Judgement.)

HS.   (Shows Sephiroth in the ז (7) Palaces.)

HS.   (Shows Sephiroth fixed to יהוה (YHVH).)

HG.   (Shows Heavens of Assiah and Averse Sephiroth.)

PATH פ (30)
Candidate is admitted by Greek Cross of יג (13) Squares

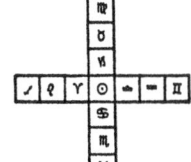

Frater Poralos enters Path פ (30)

H.   I am the ☉ (Sun) in Greatest Height.

HS.   I am the ☉ in Greatest Expression.

HG.   (As Axiokersa) I am at Equinox.

H.   (Lecture on △ (Fire).)

H.   (Explains Greek Cross and פ (30) Path= ר = Collecting Intelligence.)

H.   (Shows Key יט (19) of Tarot)

HS.   (Shows Symbols made of +○ב)

HS.   (Shows Tarot Trumps on Hebrew Letters.)

HG. (Shows Olympic Spirits)

HG. (Shows Talismans made from Geomantric Figures.)

H. I Name you Lord of ל (30th) Path.

ג = ח (3=8) CEREMONY PROPER

H. (Admit Candidate with ⚭)

HS. This is the Badge of a Stolistes. It is like the Laver of Moses and Sea of Soloman and is also △ 𝔻|O

H. (Shows diagram of Eden with ר (4) Rivers and דעת (DAATH) Eve below Adam on the ג (3)=ח (8)= הוד (HOD) and ל (30) and אל (31) Paths= ר & ש .

H. Sign 〰 =Sign ▽   הים (MEM WORD= צבאות יהוה (YHVH TZABOATH) NUMBER= אלוה   (1,30,6,8)=Forty-five. It is referred to Eighth Path=Absolutely Perfect Path. Badge is:

ג=ח (3=8) belongs to ▽ —See Watch Tower and Words EMPEH ARSEL GIAOL. On the Altar the △ is above the   =Power. Of Spirit of Life Rising above Waters and Reflecting the Triune therein. (3) ג =(8) ח Also= ☿ . See its Kamea of Sixty-four Squares. See also Sigils of ☿

ח = אנבוגה
Sixty= דיל and ידכ
Two Thousand=TAPHTPAR–HARATH=

HS. (See ☿ on Tree of Life. See ד Planes on Trees of Life. See (7) Planes on Tree of Life.)

HG. (See REsume of Planets and Alchemical ☿ on Tree of Life. of א Form.)

HI. I name you Practicus and Monokeros De Astris. I give you the Symbol) מים

H. I Proclaim you. ח = ג
Be sure to study well and make progress.

CLOSING ADVANCEMENT

H. Guard the Temple. Let us Adore the Lord and King of ▽

H. Let אלהים צבאות (ELOHIM TZABOATH) be praised.

H. (Prayer of Undines as in old MSS.)

H.

                                      Actives Passives

H. Part and may אל Bless You.

H. HS. HG. (I III I III)

ADVANCEMENT

H. Candidate is admitted with ⟁

HG. His Throne was Glame and His Wheels were as △

H. Give Sign Word. Candidate swears secrecy by the Abyss of △ call ▽ to Witness.

H. (Place Candidate before Path אֹ)

SYNONYMS IN TAROT DIVINATION

FOOL	△	11	I
HANGED MAN	▽	23	XII
JUDGEMENT	△	31	XX
JUGGLER	☿	12	II
HIGH PRIESTESS	☽	13	II
EMPRESS	♀	14	III
✪ ROTA WHEEL	♃	21	X
TOWER STRUCK BY ⚡	♂	29	XVI
SUN	☉	30	XIX
UNIVERSE	♄	32	XXI
EMPEROR	♈	15	IV
HIEROPHANT	♉	16	V
LOVERS	♊	17	VI
CHARIOT	♋	18	VII
STRENGTH (VIII)	♌	19	XI
PRUDENCE HERMIT	♍	20	IX
JUSTICE	♎	22	VIII
DEATH	♏	24	XII
TEMPERANCE	♐	25	XIV
DEVIL	♑	26	XV
STAR	♒	28	XVII
MOON	♓	29	XVIII

א ב ג ד ה ו ז ח ט י כ ל מ נ ס ע פ צ ק ר ש ת

Knowledge Necessary to pass from Practicus to Philosophus

1. Forming Planet Signs from

♄ ☿ ♃ ♄   ☽ White Nature   ☉ Red Alchemia   ⊕ Corrsn

Notice Red ♀ becomes Green.

2. ב Theory of Alchemy is Purge the Matter and Exalt it.
3. ג Alchemical Language may be Religious, or Philosophical, or Natural=Sun Mineral=Moon.
4. ד Qabalah gives Origin of All
5. ה Explain Drawing a Figure
6. ו How to Judge It
7. ז Explain Accidental Dignity
8. ח Explain Hulech–Anareta
9. ט (32 Paths in a Picture)
10. י Parts of the Soul
    ב (KETHER)=YECHIDAH
    ח (CHOCHMAH)=CHIAH
    ב (BINAH)=NESCHEMAH
    ת (TIPHARETH) AND FIVE OTHERS=RUACH
    ב (SHOULD BE   FOR MALKUTH)=NEPHESCH

11. כ Order of Angels of the (10) SEPHIROTH
    ב (KETHER) CHAIOTH HQDSH
    ח (CHOCHMAH) AUPHANIM
    ב (BINAH) ARAFIM
    ח (CHESED) CHASHMALIM
    ג (GEBURAH) SERAFIM
    ת (TIPHARETH) MELECHIM
    נ (NETZACH) ELOHIM
    ה (HOD)=BENI ELOHIM
    י (YESOD)=KERUBIM
    מ (MALKUTH)=ISHIM

12. **ס** Special Numbers and Magic Squares of the Planets
ה = ג (3)   ק = ד (4)   ♂ = ה (5)   ☉ = ו (6)
♀ = ז (7)   ☿ = ח (8)   ☽ = ט (9)

13. **ט** Names of Olympic Planetary Spirits
ARATHON–BETLOR–PHALEGH–OCH–
HAGITH–OPHIEL–PHUL.

14. **י** Mercury on The Tree of Life

15. **כ** Alchemical on The Alchemical Sephiroth

16. **ל** Planetary Symbols United in

17. **מ** Cup of Stolistes on Tree of Life

18. **נ** Cup Also= ∪○△ and מים Above and Below the Firmanent

19. **ק** Solid Greek Cross of בב (22) Squares

20. **ר** Solid Triangular Pyramid

21. **ש** Greek Cross of יג (13) Squares

22. **ת** Talismans are made from Geomantric Figures

א Intelligences of Geomantic Figures are

♈	MALCHIDEAL	♉	ASMODEL
♊	AMBRIEL	♎	ZURIEL
♏	BARAHIEL	♐	ADUACHIEL
♋	MURIEL	♌	UERCHIEL
♍	AMALIEL		
♑	HANEAL	(♓)	
♒	CAMBEL		RANNIXIEL
			MURIEL
	ZAZEL		HISMAEL
	BARTZABEL		KEDEMEL

ב Names of Genii of Planets

(4=7) PHILOSOPHUS
NOTES ON OPENING AND CLOSING
NOTES ON PATH 28.29.27.

Philosophus ד = ז 4=7

Three months have passed in the Grade if Practicus

ד = ז Sit in the East.

Grade belongs to אש Fire and to ♀ and to נצח (NETZACH). To Open Chatechise as usual and in Closing recite Prayer of the Salamander. Open and Close in the Name of יהוה צבאות . (JEHOVAH TZABOATH).

The Paths are כצ(29) כח (28) כז (27). Each in full before the Ceremony of ז= ד

(4)=(7) Philosophus
Includes Paths כצ(29) כח(28) כז(27)
and then ד = ז (4=7) Proper
Open in Temple of Path כצ (29)

H.	(Finds all is secure and only ד = ז (4=7) are present.)
HG.	△
HS.	♀
HS.	(Paths are כט(29)כח (28) כז (27)
H.	What is Path כט (29)?
HG.	♓ (Pisces). The reflection of ♒ (Aquarius) is כח (28) כז (27)=Reflection of ♂ (Mars)
H.	Adoration of יהוה צבאות (IHVH TZABOATH)
H.	(Calls on אלהים (ELOHIM–Michael. OIP TEAA PEDOCE EDELPEPNA. Making ☽ ✶ ✶ ✶
H.	(I III I III)
HS.	(I III I III)
HG.	(I III I III)

CLOSING

H.	(Sees to Guard and to Rank of those present.)
H.	(Adoration to Lord of △)
H.	(Speaks Salamandrine Prayer as in Ancient MSS.)
H.	(Dismisses SALS in Name of יהוה צבאות (IHVH TZABOATH)
H.	(I II III)
HS.	(I II III)
HG.	(I II III)

CLOSE PASSIVES ACTIVES BANISH △

PATH בט (29)

H. (Gives notice of A ג = ה (3=8)

H. (Admits with ✝ Blinded

The ג = ה (3=8) gives Signs and Words. Mystic Title and Symbols of ▽ is then pledged and swears by △. Light restored.

HE. (Waves Incense and is put in East and is shewn Portals of לא (31) לב (32) בט (29) Paths. Once round H. stops with Red Lamp as OSIRUS as Stagnant ▽ –stopped by HS. as HORUS As Turbid Troubled ▽ –stopped by HG as ISIS as Pure ▽ .)

H. (Speaks to ג = ה (3=8) as Lord of All Waters.

H. (Explains the Calvary ✝ of יב (12) Squares= Zodiac. Embracing NU and also River of Eden which divides into ד (4) Heads. Path בט (29)=is the Corporeal Intelligence and refers to Pisces. By it the Waters of חסד (CHESED) flow down.)

H. (Points out on Altar the יב (12th) Key of the Tarot

Note the Two Lunas
Crayfish Cancer Scarab
Kephra

H. (Then shows Nehushtan the Mosaic Serpent

שרפים (SERAPHIM)
Type of Christ
Brass= ♀ Venus= נוגה (NOGAH)

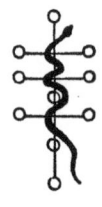

HS. (Shows Qaballah of ט (9) Chambers) in ב (2) forms and the Tree of Life in the Tarot.)

HG. (Shows diagram of Three Pillars and Talismans made from Geomantric Figures.)

H. (I name you Lady or Lord of the כט (29th) Path.

PATH כט (29)
Candidate is admitted by Bade of a Solid Pyramid

HG. The Rivers of Eden flow from a Central Source.

The ג (3) Circumambulations

H. (With Lamp I am Rain Cherisher and Harvest Wielder. I am Isis.

HS. I am Nephthys+Dew

HG. I am Athor=Mist=Cloud of Autumn

H. HS. HG. Recite sentences of Zoro about the Monad and Duad and Fountains and Matrix and Matter.)

H. (Describes △.)

H. The כה (28) Path= צ Natural Intelligence and ♒ = Man=The Adam=Restored World.

H. (Shows Key יז (17) of Tarot)
Sirius ה = ♀ = Isis
♒ = מים (MEM) at her Feet.

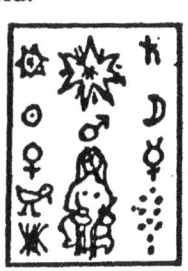

Path כן (27)

Is admitted by ⊥┬⊥ י (10) Squares

HG. By River Kishon Go in Name of Lord of Armies

H. (Recites Kabbalistic View of Creation–Edom Kings)

H. (Gives Judges כ – ה about Kishon)

HG. (Continues)

HS. Habbakkuk ג – ג

H. (Explains ⊥┬⊥ Path = Exciting Intelligence)

H. (Shows Key=Tower of Babel)

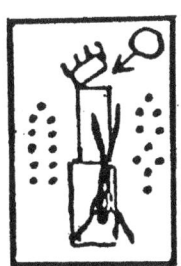

H. (Shows ⚨ on Tree of Life)

H. (Shows on Tree of Life)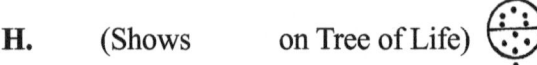

HS. (Shows Trinity)

HG. (Shows Image of Nebuchadnazzer)

HG. (Shows Name of Forty-two Letters in ז (7) Palaces of י (10) Sephiroth.)

HG. (Shows Qlippoth and Twelve Princes.)

H. Rise Lady or Lord of Path ז

CEREMONY OF ד = ז (4=7)

ז is admitted by  Badge of HS

H. (Explains it)

HS. (Explains a Picture of the Fall. The Goddess who is supporter is Fallen and with Her Adam Microprosopus–Great Dragon arose. Second Adam is needed.)

THIS ד = ז (4=7) = פלסופ = נצח

SIGN= 🤝 = △ =Fire

WORD= יהוה צבאות (YHVH TZABOATH)
To this ז (7) Path of Yetzirah-Recondite Intelligence.

Badge= [diagram of badge]

ד = ז (4=7) Belongs to △ –H. Shows Fire Tablet.

See–OIP TEEA PEDOCE

H. (On Altar see ⌬ = ⌬ Sulphur)

H. (Shows Kamea of Forty-Nine Squares.)

THE FALL (4=7)

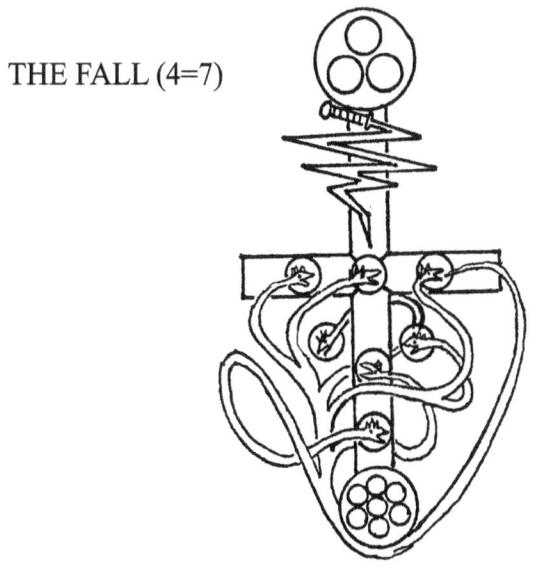

ADEPT'S JEWEL

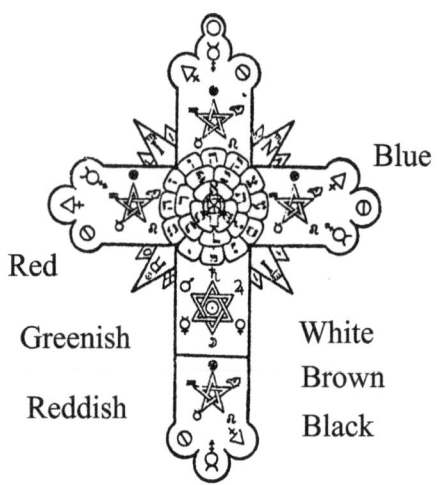

Blue
Red
Greenish
White
Brown
Reddish
Black

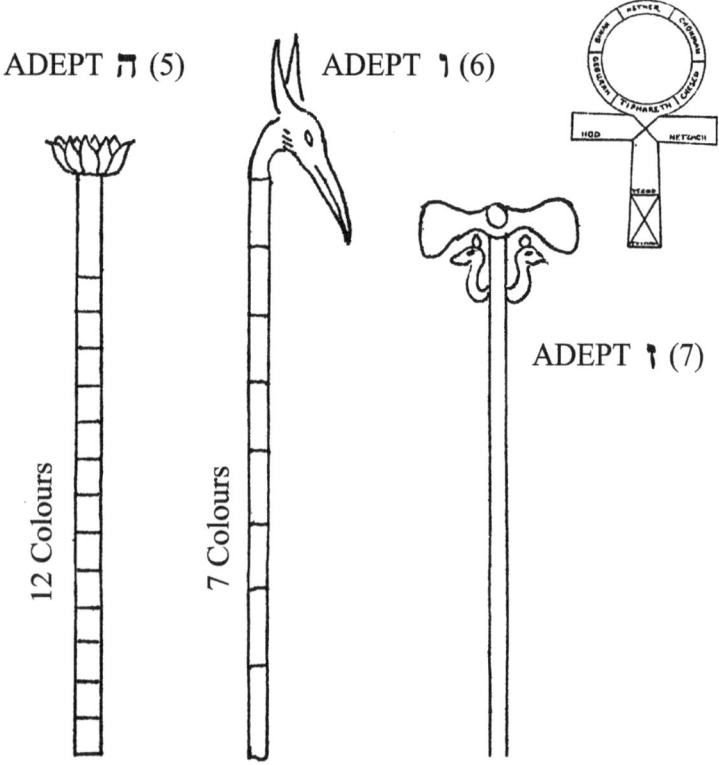

ADEPT ה (5)

ADEPT ו (6)

ADEPT ז (7)

12 Colours

7 Colours

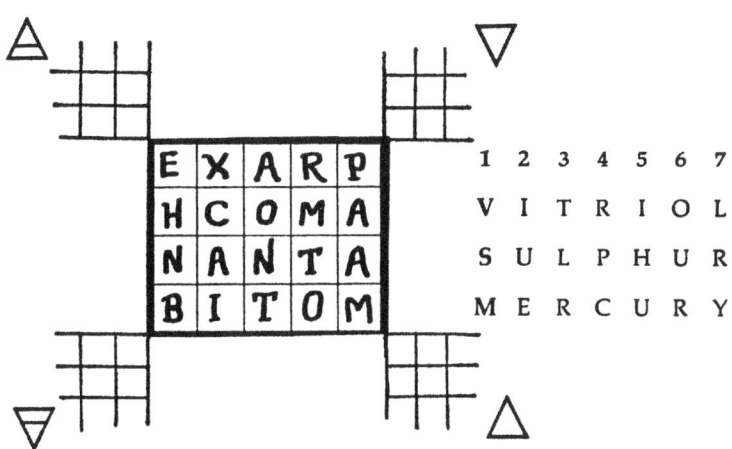

```
       1  2  3  4  5  6  7
       V  I  T  R  I  O  L
       S  U  L  P  H  U  R
       M  E  R  C  U  R  Y
```

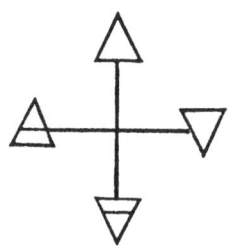

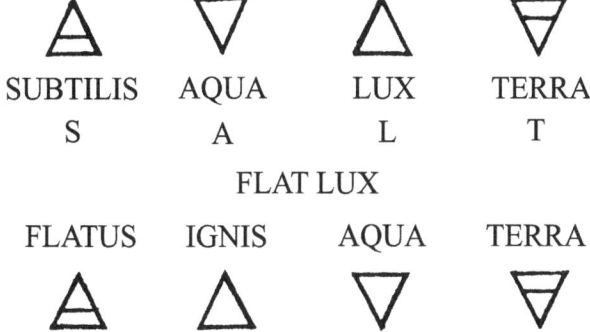

SUBTILIS   AQUA   LUX   TERRA
   S   A   L   T
           FLAT LUX
 FLATUS   IGNIS   AQUA   TERRA

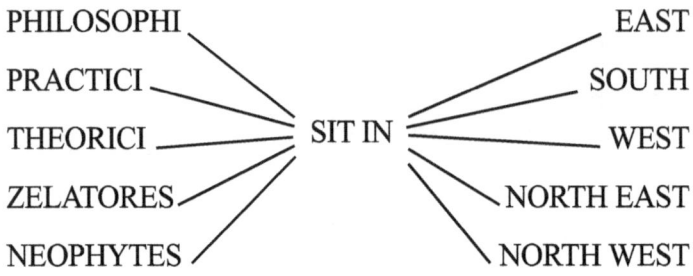

Adepts sit on raised place with the Hierophant. Incense should be burning in the Temple at all Ceremonies. Three Chiefs each ה (5)= ו (6) should hold a Temple one of whom must be present at all Ceremonies. Officers change every ו (6) months.

Avoid Roman Catholics but with Pity.

See Sigils of אהא =

   חגיאל (HAGIEL)

   קדמאל (KEDEMEL)

   בני שרפים (BENI SERAPHIM)

H.	(Shows ♀ on Tree of Life)
HS.	(Shows Path with דעת (DAATH).)
HS.	(Shows Tablets of Sephiroth in Worlds.)
HG.	(Shows Solomon's Altar.)
HG.	(Shows Brazen Sea.)
H.	I name you Pharos Illuminans and אש△ פרת
H.	(Exorts to study and call Her or Him Honoured.)

END OF FIRST ORDER

CHAPTER 3

THE GODS AND RITUAL

"There is no part of me that is not of the Gods" was a favorite saying of Mathers, which was paraphrased from the *Book of the Dead*. It showed his aspirations in attaining Adeptship. In the Golden Dawn, godforms from various cultures were considered as currents or potencies of energies that could be tapped and directed to perform a desired task. A good example of this tapping of energy is given in the signs of the 5=6 Grade in which the Adept draws down the powers of forces which are synthesized into a specific current of energy. The first time this appears to any great extent is in the 5=6 Grade where the Adept is filled with the energy needed to be able to perform the task about to be initiated. The following paper, by Dr. R. Felkin, was issued to Whare Ra members once they achieved the 5=6 rank. It explains this from a slightly subjective, though nevertheless interesting viewpoint.

DR. FELKIN'S NOTES ON THE DIVINE WHITE BRILLIANCE (D.W.B.)

All effective ritual is a condensed drama of Life. And Life again is a compendium of the cosmic drama. A ceremony, if it be true, must correspond to the great cosmic pageant of creative evolution and involution.

True occult ritual is one of the great harmonizing agents, because by representing the cosmic acts it brings them into closer relation with human life. Even a very brief and simple ritual for helping those in trouble or sickness must conform to this Law if it is to be effectual. That is why the L.V.X. signs and invocation of the D.W.B. is so remarkable in its results. It is an epitome of the Redemption. Just consider it in detail and you will realize this.

We begin by intoning the letters I.N.R.I. We recall the varied significance attributed to these letters—Jesus Nazarenus Rex Judicorum. It is, of course, a form of the 4-fold Name (Yod He Vau He), but its essential significance is not creative but redemptive. The Sun in Virgo accomplishing the transmutation of Scorpio. The Virgin Mother treading on the head of the Serpent that the Father may be born anew in the Son. It is the Key to the whole Rosicrucian philosophy, the redemption of Matter, transforming the human into the Divine. The blending of the dew and fire in purification and consecration. The exaltation of the Cross of Light.

So, from the four we pass to three—the triangle of Spirit rising from the cube of Matter. Isis the eternal virgin (under whatever name we hail her: Eternal Mother, Sophia, Mary); Osiris, Father, and Son Jesus. And between them the Serpent which must be transformed into the eagle. The destroyer who must become the transmuter.

Remember that these three letters have a further significance thus: "I" stands for the ego, the indestructible unit which survives from life to life. "O" is the eternal Spirit, embracing the Universe, reaching out beyond the boundaries of time and space, yet revolving about the "I." And between them the "A" of the Astral, the veil of perpetually shifting illusion and experience. I–A –O. Man–Cosmos–God. From their union issues forth the Divine White Brilliance, the Cross of Light, healing, redeeming, illuminating.

Some years ago when I was first initiated into the R.R. et A.C. by Jack Taylor, I found myself at loggerheads with the Christian viewpoint in interpreting these energies because of its limitations. Not being a denominational Christian in the mundane sense of the word, yet being among a group of elderly devotees who considered this part and parcel of their whole existence, did have its problems. A good example of this emerged when at 5=6 level I was informed that Mrs. Felkin taught that the Inner Order Grades of the Golden Dawn were Christian. Some twenty years previous, I had studied Tantra and Yantric meditational methods under the late Vivandatta, who taught me the value of the personal and the impersonal nature of the godforms. From this, I believe that Mrs. Felkin and some others were mistaken in this concept as they no doubt accepted Christ as their personal saviour. Any Christian will tell you that Christ has to be first and accepts no other gods before Him. The Cosmic attribution of Christ however, is an entirely different matter and can be taken into Order teachings with just as much fervor as a personal one.

The way I got around this was to accept that Christ was the office held and Jesus was the man in that office. Christ epitomizes suffering and redemption through trial and tribulation and as such is a very potent force to invoke; this is the energy we call on in the R.R. et A.C. when we use His name. One of the best archetypal concepts I have ever seen was in Crowley's Trump: the Magus which showed the Crucified Christ analogous to Mercury.

If we take another look at the D.W.B. formulae, it becomes blatantly obvious that the godforms called upon represent different currents of energies. These energies had not previously been rationalized on any reasonable basis within the Golden Dawn. Within the New Zealand Order though, these energies are dissected and categorized as component parts in much the same way one peels off the layers of an onion. This type of approach is needed, as some of the rituals and practices of the G.D. are extremely complex, with a great deal more revelation required concerning hidden meanings.

An example of this is from the 5=6 ritual when I.N.R.I. is discussed:

> **The Keyword is I.N.R.I., which is inscribed with its correspondences upon this complete symbol of the Rose and Cross which I bear upon my breast.** These letters have been occasionally used as the initials of the following sentences: JESUS NAZARENUS REX JUDECORUM, whence it symbolizes the Grand Word which is YEHESHUA or the Hebrew

Name of Jesus, formed of the Holy letters Shin, representing the Ruach Elohim, placed within the Centre of the Name Tetragrammaton. Also it has been interpreted as: Igne Natura Renvatur Integra; Igne Natura Renovando Integrat; Igne Nitrum Roris Invenitur; Intra Nobles Regnum Dei.

From a personal viewpoint, the first of these interpretations seems to be the most powerful and within Order concepts. Whatever one has to say about Christ, all will agree that His Name evokes a powerful current or force that fills us with the receptive principle, something akin to the Yin of Chinese metaphysics. This principle of receptivity is one that is needed, for when we invoke it, we pave the way for the forces, fused together, to enter our sphere of sensation. The Christ-like energy will pacify and control it, so that it conforms to our will and can be directed for many different uses. It must also be stressed here that we invoke the energy of resurrection and immortality. Something necessary for us to equate with the Osirian concept of the 5=6 energy.

The first real fusion of energies within the 5=6 comes with the phrase, "Virgo, Isis, Mighty Mother." This is issued by the Chief Adept which shows the framework it is derived from in Chesed, the Sephiroth of Mercy. All the associations to Chesed are now evoked from, and linked to, our personalized sphere of Chesed within our bodies. The phrase "Scorpio, Apophis, Destroyer" relates to the Sephirah of Geburah, and the strength and security that is associated with it through the Second Adept. So far, we have called on two extremes. To call down either would be asking for trouble, but the Christ energy of I.N.R.I. synthesizes it safely into a powerful force of even balance and polarity. The phrase, "Sol, Osiris, Slayen and Risen" uttered by the Third Adept, now equates us with transferring that energy into the direct sphere of Man, Guph, the physical body; but with new vitality. Sol is the energy of the Sun, while Osiris is the renewed form of life.

The DWB, as it is called down, in fact works through the various subtle body layers and hence a resurgence of vitality is experienced. The energy of the Sun, and a resurrected Osiris, is considered limitless. What limits there are, are self imposed and have to be peeled away like the layers of an onion. The final saying in fact personalizes the Cosmic Christ concept down to a level that we can understand and direct, in accordance with Order teaching methods. The final phrasing now calls on our auric bodies to open wider these channels of operation, while the formula IAO (pronounced and fully vibrated as EEEE AAAA OOOO), is likened to a switch to bring down this energy in its fullest capacity.

The IAO formula is almost as complex as that of I.N.R.I. Modern Kabbalistic scholars such as Scholem, have indicated that the IAO could possibly be a corrupt version of Jao, a Greek rendition of IAU TzBAUTh taken from the Lesser Hekhaloth text. This also could equate to the godname of the Sephirah of Netzach. There is also evidence that the IAO was also an alchemical process whose meaning has been lost with time. The current Order teaching considers that IAO fuses the Isis, Apophis and Osiris energies together into one workable formula, being at the hands of the Adept to direct for a specific purpose.

In the 5=6 Ritual, the Adept first experiences godform assumption when lashed to the cross of suffering; and later in the role of the Chief Adept in the pastos, who assumes the astral body of the Postulant, and later when the Postulant holds the crook and scourge of Osiris.

The energies of the various godforms, plus the rituals and props, amount to what could be described as a mass attack on the psyche of the individual. Those who go through the 5=6 Ceremony with full props, will experience changes in their lives. Some experience a dramatic shock then and there during the Ceremony itself, while others noticed changes in themselves months after. All agree that the 5=6 Ritual with its evocative powers can change one's life. Over the years, I have had the opportunity of speaking with dozens of Adepts who underwent the 5=6 Ceremony at Whare Ra and within the Thothe Hermes Temple. Its effects can be roughly categorized into two levels: the first is when there is shutdown in magical work. These people have only consecrated their elemental weapons and do little else save attend the Equinox Ceremony. I am sure that their psyches produce this effect because their psyches cannot cope with any more magical work, for a variety of reasons. The other level is completely opposite; the energies are opened up and can totally exhaust one if the framework and structure of the grade is not adhered to.

In an instance that I can recall, one person underwent the 5=6 Ceremony at Whare Ra in the 1950s, and spent the next six years in a mental institution. He was in fact warned by Jack Taylor not to take this grade. Jack by his clairvoyance correctly deduced that this person was not ready for the 5=6 energy, but he went ahead with the Ceremony anyway. Today, he has virtually no recollection of his 5=6 Grade or any of his magical studies, except for an inner fear when the subject is broached. It was because of this negative effect that the 5=6 can produce that the old 5=6 curriculum of Whare Ra was never introduced into the Thothe Hermes Temple. Instead, a newer one was drafted up that took the Adept step-by-step through the various levels.

The following paper by Mathers was one of the few that he did on the symbolism of the 5=6 Grade and the Outer Order symbolism; it is highly significant:

Concerning the Symbolism of Self Sacrifice, and Crucifixion contained in the 5=6 Grade by G.H. Frater D.D.F.C.

This lecture was delivered on Good Friday, March 31, 1893, to the Adept College Assembled.

Dealing first of all with the diagrams in the first Order and proceeding upwards, it will be noticed that in the lowest Grade in the Outer (0=0) there are no diagrams, properly so called, but that on the two Pillars is depicted the symbolism of the passage of the soul from the Egyptian Ritual of the Dead; this being as it were a sympathetic aspect to be developed and explained with the advance of the candidate through the various stages.

After the first Grade comes the 1=10, where we find the first form of the Sephiroth in the Tree of Life; this is the representation of the flaming Sword descending, but it is not until the 2=9 comes that we begin to find the actual Symbol of Self Sacrifice. The 2=9 Altar Diagram, then, represents the Serpent of Wisdom twined through the Paths. In the 4=7 Grade however, you are shown the same Serpent; its representation being that of Serpent Nechushtan. This was the Serpent of Brass that Moses made in the Wilderness, and which was turned around the central Pillar of Mildness, having three cross bars upon it, representing a species of triple cross.

Dealing now with the Altar Diagram of the 3=8 Grade, it will be seen that Adam is the

Tiphareth part, wherein he is extended. That is say that the form of the man is projected from there.

The figure of Eve stands in Malkuth, in the form of the Supporter.

The first ideal form of Man is in Adam Kadmon, behind the Kether form and, as it were, the prototype of the Tiphareth form. This Tiphareth answers to the letter Vau of the Holy Name, as representing the Prince. The letter Vau also represents the number Six and Adam was created on the Sixth day, for Tiphareth is the Symbol of the Creation. Furthermore, the Hexagram consists of the two forms Fire and Water: the ideal Fire and the ideal Water; the Spirit and the Water of Creation; the spiritual Ether and the Ethereal Fire; the Fire of the Holy Spirit. Thus, in the creation of the Man is the extension from Tiphareth i.e., the moment Adam is created, that is the beginning of the reflection of the lower Triad, and finally, of Malkuth. Eve is the synthesis of Creation and represents the Mother of Life, as the name Cha VaH. The 3=8 diagram thus represents the establishment of life, i.e., created life, and it is the Tree of Knowledge of Good and Evil, because it is the balance point between Good and Evil; for in the material body we are placed to give victory to which we will. Hence the significance of the Serpent, "Ye shall be as Gods, knowing Good and Evil." But the knowledge of Evil brought with it the descent into the Qlippoth, and although Malkuth is directly involved in the "fall," the Sephiroth immediately above cannot be said to have actually entered into the Knowledge of Evil. Therefore, in the allegorical account of the Creation in Genesis, it is said that Man is checked from putting forth his hand to take of the Tree of Life, so as not to involve the higher Sephiroth in the "Fall" which, (he being unbalanced in himself) would only have precipitated disaster.

In the 4=7 diagram we find represented the Fall and the consequent rise of the Dragon, which in the 3=8 Grade is represented coiled beneath Malkuth in the Kingdom of the Shells; but it only raises its head to the Sephiroth by right of the Crowns of the Kings of Edom.

These latter represent the Worlds of unbalanced force, before the Creation is established. Furthermore, they symbolize the places of the Sephiroth which are hollowed, and before the light fills the cavities (the Light which comes down and fills the cavities is to be found allegorically set forth in the story of the usurpation of the younger brother in the story of Esau and Jacob), "before all things were the Waters, and the Darkness, and the Gates of the Land of Night." Note also the War of the Titans who rise and fight against Jupiter.

The Edomite Kings therefore, are not altogether Evil. They are the forces of restriction.

The result therefore, on a higher plane in the Tree, is that the Great serpent rises to Daath, and the Four Worlds balanced upon the Tree itself, it will be observed that the cutting off by the Serpent is between Yetziirah and Briah. Thus, Evil cannot arise into the World of Briah, or indeed transcend the limits of Yetzirah. But if we seek for the correspondence of Evil in the Worlds of Briah and Atziluth, it will be found to consist in a lesser form of Good: a limiting, restricting and binding force without which you cannot have form on the higher planes. It is only in the Worlds of Yetzirah and Assiah that the analogue of this principle becomes absolutely Evil.

This idea was first expressed by the Gnostics, when they said that Achamoth attempted to comprehend the Pleroma, but could not understand it, and from the grief of her were formed the demons and evil spirits.

If therefore we seek to institute an analogy concerning the Microcosm, it will be seen the Nephesch refers to Malkuth and Assiah; Ruach will refer to Yetzirah, which is the World of Formation. Therefore, the formative principle operating in the Ruach gives form to all ideas, and is that which weighs, balances and works in things. Ruach can also have an evil side.

Neschamah is equated with the higher aspirations of the Soul, which aspires to the ideal. There can be no positive evil side to Neschamah. There will be only a higher or lower aspiration.

If the Ruach overpowers the Neschamah; if the Neschamah seeks the lower good: both will be ruined. The following of a false idea cannot be said to be exactly evil, but is a lower Good than it should be.

Neschamah will answer to the World of Briah, so also will Chiah, which is allotted to Chokmah; but you cannot touch the Yechidah part of you with your Ruach: you must use the consciousness of the Neschamah. This Yechidah will, together with Chiah, be the "Higher Genius," though this again will not be the highest self. For in and behind Kether will reside a part of the being, which it is impossible to understand, and which one can only aim at: this is the highest Soul, and answering to the highest part of Yechidah, cannot be touched by Neschamah. There must be a mode of transferring the synthesis of the consciousness making up Man to this upper Sephirah. The fall, which cut away the Higher from the lower Sephiroth in Daath, was also our descent into this life, as it were, from that Upper and Higher Soul. Therefore, our objective is to get into contact with that again, which is only to be done through the Neschamah, which is Divine Mother of the Soul: our Aima.

When the Candidate enters the Vault and kneels down at the second point, during the 5=6 Ceremony, he does so at the centre of the Altar above the symbolic form of the Adept, who is the synthesis of the sides of the Vault, from whence he has come forth. He occupies a central position between Kether and the World of Shades, being there protected by the rising glory of the Golden Cross and the Rose. Then this Prayer is said: *"Unto Thee Sole Wise, Sole Mighty and Sole Eternal One, be Praise and Glory forever."* Now it must be the Macroposopus, the Amen, who is addressed here; The Lord of Kether, who has permitted this Aspirant who now kneeleth before Him to penetrate thus far into the Sanctuary of His Mysteries, (which is in the centre of the Universe). *"Not unto us, but unto His Name be Glory"* (which is the name YHVH, with the addition of the letter Shin). "Let the influence of Thy Divine Ones descend upon his head," (These Divine Ones are Angelic forces, and the Higher Self is that of the Divine One) "and teach him the value of self sacrifice, so that he shall shrink not in the hour of trial, but that thus; His name may be written on high" (that is, the Divine name formulated in him may be brought up, as it were, to the heights), "and may stand in the presence of the Holy One" (which genius will be a might Angelic power, and in a form far different from the petty personages we are here); "in that hour, when the Son of man is invoked before the Lord of Spirits, and His name, in the Presence of the Ancient Days."

This will be the synthetical form of the Son of Man, the Ben Adams, who is the synthesis of the Ruach of the Universe in other words, the allusion is to the Great God of the World of Yetzirah or the Microprosopus, the Son of the first Adam when He is invoked before the Lord of Spirits, which can but be in Kether; and His Name in the presence of the Ancient of Days. "He who is ancient before the Gods, ancient before time, ancient before the formation of the Worlds, He the ETERNAL AMEN, or even He who is before Amen, and whom the plumes of Amen's headdress only touch."

Now the foregoing partly represents the mode in which the initiate becomes the Adept: the Ruach, directed in accordance with the promptings of the Neschamah, keeps the Nephesch from being the ground of the Evil forces, and the Neschamah brings the Ruach into contact with the Chiah, i.e., the genius which stands in the presence of the Holy One–the Yechidah–the Divine self; which stands, as it were, before the Synthetical God of all things. That is the only real way to become the Greatest Adept, and is directly dependent on your life and your actions in life.

And upon the lid of the Pastos this process is symbolically resumed: there we see the suffering Man, pitiful and just, before whose injustice and purity the heads of the dragon fall back, but on the upper half there is depicted a tremendous and a flaming God, the fully initiated Man: the Adept who has attained his Supreme Initiation.

It will be noticed that in the 4=7 Diagram the heads of the Dragon have seized the Sephiroth but, as before remarked, on the lid of the Pastos they are falling back from the figure on the Cross: they are dispossessed only by the sacrifice of the lower Self.

Recall to your mind that passage in one of the Eddas: "I hung on the Tree three days and three nights, wounded with spear, myself, a sacrifice offered to my (highest) Self: Odin unto Odin." It will furthermore be noticed that this way of looking at the matter at once makes a reconciliation between the account in the Gospel of the Christ as a calm, peaceful, and pitiful man, and the representation in the Apocalype of a tremendous and flaming God. A glance at the top half of the Pastos shows the descent of a flaming sword which casts out evil, the whole surrounding being with brilliance. "And He had in his right hand Seven Stars...and the Seven Stars represent the (Arch) Angels of the Seven Churches," or abodes in Assiah, at his feet...

The Life of Nations is like the life of men: they are born, become intellectual, direct that intellect to black ends, and perish. But every now and then, at the end of certain periods, there are greater crises in the World's history than at other periods. At such times it becomes necessary that Sons of Gods should be incarnated to lead on the new era of the Universe. I do not affirm that Christ was necessarily a man who obtained Adeptship in that incarnation, but rather one who had obtained Adeptship and had come down to be incarnated again to lead up the new era. It was however, necessary in the crucifixion of so great a Soul, that the form might actually suffer; that everything except the Nephesch, which was temporarily abandoned in this case, was the cloak of that incarnation. In other words, only through the mortal part about the Man or the God, (and then only after incurring that physical death, as it were), could the other divine parts suddenly come down and make it the resurrected or glorified body, which, according to description, had after the Resurrection, the apparent solidity of the ordinary body, and the faculties of the Spirit Body. Because if you can once get the great force of the Highest to send its ray clean down through the Neschamah into the mind, and thence into our physical body, the Pehesch would be so transformed as to render you almost like a God walking this Earth.

The Ruach, the, has to undergo a certain check and suffering in order to attain its Apotheosis, which is the work of our Adept.

In the fully initiated Adept, the Nephesch is so withdrawn into the Ruach, that even the lowest parts of these two principles cease to become allied to the body and are drawn into the first six Sephiroth. This is again brought out in the Obligation, where you say, "I pledge myself to hereby give myself to the Great Work, which is so to exalt my lower nature that I may at length become more human, and thus gradually raise and unite myself and Divine genius." If it is a very great thing to unite yourself to the genius, how much more so if must be to unite yourself to the God that is behind it!

Looking at the Pastos, it will be seen that it represents a kind of triple cube, the whole of which is placed between light and darkness. The Lid is half Light and half Darkness: the upper end is the symbol of Light, and the lower, the symbol of Darkness; while the sides have the colours placed between the Light and the Darkness. At the head is placed a Golden Greek cross representing the Spirit and the Elements, and a Rose of 7 times 7 petals, and four rays which go out from it. But at the foot, that which the feet rest on as if they were exalted by it, is the Cross exalted on a pedestal of Three Steps: the Obligation Cross. This latte is also to an extent represented on the top in the crucified figure, and symbolizes the voluntary sacrifice of the lower will, which is incidental to allaying the intellect with the higher aspirations, and to the establishment of your consciousness therein: thus, if the ordinary consciousness were centered in the Ruach, you could touch the Neschamah, while if it was in the latter, you could touch the Genius.

Now this tranference of consciousness from Ruach to Neschamah is one object of the ceremony of the 5=6 Ritual: it is a thing which will be more readily understood when the Grade of Adeptus Minor is reached. It is especially intended to effect the change of consciousness into the Neschamah, and there are places where it can take place. The first is when the Aspirant is on the Cross, because he is so exactly fulfilling the symbol of the abnegation of the lower self and the union with the Higher Self; there is also the invocation of the Angel H.U.A.

The second place is when he touches the Rose of the representative of C.R. in the Vault, when he has taken on himself the symbols of suffering and self sacrifice, and says that his victory is in the Cross of the Rose.

The third place is when he enters the Vault in the third point and kneels down, and the Chief Adept say "I am the reconciler with the Ineffable: I am the dweller of the invisible: let the White Brilliance of the Divine Spirit descend."

In these three cases a possible exchange of consciousness from the Ruach into the Neschamah is initiated, so that whether he understands it or not, the Aspirant actually approaches his own Genius. (There are some cases where the Genius may have attained a height and fallen; that is when, having touched the Ruach in one incarnation, it has been so wrought upon by sufferings of the lower part, that it has for the moment consented to slaken the tension of their union. Now if the Genius part, instead of identifying itself with the God part, identifies itself too much with the Neschamah, a fall of the Genius takes place; this is not altogether evil, but may entail a certain evil effect.)

The most complete point of actual contact is in the third point, where the Chief Adept says: "I am the Resurrection and the Life! He that believeth in me, though he were dead, yet shall he live, and whosoever liveth and believeth in me shall never die": i.e., if you can live at will in the Neschamah and touch of the Genius, you will have made a great step towards the Divine Elixer, for you will be worthy to sit with the Gods, and that which you drink of is real Elixer of the Spirit of Life.

Then the Second Adept says: "Behold the Image of the Justified One, crucified on the Cross of the Infernal Rivers of Death," and the Third Adept shows deific antithesis: the exaltation into the Divine. Then the Chief Adept says again: "I am the First and the Las," (the Adept and the Tau and the Yod and the HeH(f) of the sacred Name), "I am He that liveth but was dead, and behold I am alive for evermore, Amen"; that is using the name of the Egyptian Deity AMON, (or Amen), who represents the Ideal God Force, "and I hold the Keys of Death and of Hell." (Because if you stand on Malkuth and keep your touch with the Gods, you hold the Keys of that which is below.)

But the lower self all this time has an existence, for it certainly is not quite eliminated: it is cast forth from the Nephesch, yet preserving a link with it, it goes down into the Qlippoth, and in this connection, it is well to observe what may really be Evil on this Earth plane, may be even as a God among the Demons. the words "He descendeth into Hell," have such a significance.

This Third point then represents the attainment of the Divine. The Second Adept proceeds to say: "He that hath an ear let him hear what the Spirit says unto the Assemblies" (i.e., in Malkuth), and if the Voice of the Divine is found in Malkuth, it must find its echo in the realms beneath.

Then follows the exaltation into Neschamah of the Consciousness of the Chief Adept, whose

Voice seems as if he were symbolically standing with his head in Atziluth, whence it reverberates through the Worlds, sinking down below Malkuth unto the dominion of the Shells, and he says: "For I know that my Redeemer liveth" (the Redeemer is He that brings again), "and that He shall stand at the latter day upon the Earth. I am the Way, the Truth, and the Life. No Man cometh unto the Father but by me." This whole passage of the Chief Adept is formed of a collection of utterances, which are, as it were, the speeches of the Great Gods, which he can only hear when he is still further exalted into Kether. "I am the Way, the Truth, and the Life," is the reflected Triad. No man cometh unto the Father, but by me. Then the Neschamah speaks down to "I have entered into the Invisible." Then it is as if the Consciousness went into the Genius, which says "I am the Sun in his rising, I have passed through the hour of the Cloud and Night."

Then follows: "I am Amon the Concealed One, the Opener of Day," like the Great God in Atziluth, "I am Osiris Onnofris, the Crucified One," who is perfected in the balance and rise above all considerations that cometh from Maya, or illusion, and who only seeks the eternal life from above, and then, as if in a supreme moment "I am the Lord of Life, triumphant over death, and there is no part of me that is not of the Gods." (That is the Voice of Kether.) This again is followed by a synthetical culmination, as if all the Divine ones united in the utterance: "I am the Preparer of the pathway, the rescuer unto the Light! Out of the Darkness let the Light arise!"

Then the Aspirant is prompted to say: "Before, I was blind, but now I see," representing again the blindness to the Neschamah Consciousness and the passage into this.

Whereupon the Chief Adept says: "I am the Reconciler with the Ineffable! I am the dweller of the invisible; let the White Brilliance of the Divine Spirit descend."

The Aspirant is now told to rise an Adeptus Minor of the Rose of Ruby and the Cross of Gold, in the sign of Osiris Slain; and then, "We receive thee as Adeptus Minor in that sign of Osiris Slain; and then, "We receive thee as Adeptus Minor in that sign of rectitude and Self Sacrifice."

The affirmation of three parts is then proceeded with: The Chief Adept says: "Be thy mind opened unto the Higher," (Second Adept), "Be thy heart the centre of Light," (Third Adept), "Be thy body the temple of the Rosy Cross."

The Pass Word is then announced, which is formed from the Mystic Number of the Grade: 21. This Pass Word, however, is the Divine Name of Kether: it is used as the Pass Word of this Grade of Tiphareth in order to affirm the connection between the two.

Then the Chief Adept says that the Key Word is I.N.R.I. The three Adepts themselves represent Chesed, Geburah and Tiphareth. The Creator, the Destroyer and the Sacrificed One: ISIS, APOPHIS and OSIRIS equals the IAO. The Symbol of Osiris Slain is the Cross; vis, the Sign of the Mourning of Isis: the sign of Typhon and Apophis: X the sign of Osiris Risen:=LVX the Light of the Cross, or that which symbolizes the way into the Divine through Sacrifice. So that the symbolism in it entirety represents the exaltation of the Initiate into the Adept...

The above paper by Mathers shows the complexity of the energies employed within the 5=6 Grade and gives some indication of the variation of energies one has to be able to recognize and control.

By now it will become obvious to those who study both the Outer Order and Inner Order rituals that there are six major currents or levels of energies applied during ritual. These are the currents of: Thoth, Isis, Horus, Nephthys, Osiris, and Christ. These can be fused together when needed to produce a very potent force, with the currents of the minor godforms working under the man ones. All other side potencies of energies take a back seat to these energies, because it is they who give the other powers a chance to operate during ritual. How this comes about can be best explained in a speech from the Neophyte Ritual:

> **Let the number of the Officers in this degree and the nature of their Offices be proclaimed once again, that the powers whose images they are may be re-awakened in the Spheres of those present, and in the sphere of this Order; for by the names and images are all powers awakened and re-awakened.**

This speech by the Hierophant gives the whole concept of Golden Dawn Ritual work. The main effort for the Adept is to discern and record what energies govern what areas of what ceremonies.

The published rituals of the Golden Dawn give only the barest hint as to what exactly happens in ceremonies like the Neophyte. Jack Taylor revealed to us that before each Grade Ceremony, the Hierophant had to go down to the Temple, and with his Sphere of Sensation (aura), link directly into the Astral Shells of each of the godforms in the rituals. Taking the 0=0 as an example, the Hierophant would have to "bring through" the Astral Shells of: (1) the Invisible Stations, (2) the Officers of the Temple, and (3) the Osiris godform on the Dias. This is an example of the verbal information that the former Hierophant would divulge, and show to the present Hierophant (providing the present never held the Hierophant position before), after the Equinox Ceremony. This practice was not restricted to a particular grade, but to the "Office." Some of those Hierophants who were 6=5 or 7=4, and who never held the position before, might be shown this by a Hierophant of, for example, the 5=6 Grade.

It must be also considered that while the Stella Matutina had quite a few shortcomings, practical ritual (within the New Zealand Order at least) was not one of them. The Golden Dawn only had a functioning Outer Order for no more than 12 years (from 1888 to 1900), while the Inner Order lasted eight years (1892-1900). It is also quite obvious that the Z-1 and Z-3 clairvoyant descriptions of the Neophyte Ceremony were done very early, possibly within about three years or so of the first Neophyte Ceremony, and left very little for further evaluations.

Within the Stella Matutina for example, they had another 70 years of life, and a number of those who were clairvoyant had the opportunity to test their theories and pass this information onto those they trained. What a lot of writers seem to forget is that the Stella Matutina was, in its beginning, made up of Golden Dawn Adepti trained by Mathers, Florence Farr, and others of equal notoriety. It did not, at 1900 suddenly cease to exist and redirect its magical power. It had a wealth of unpublished information to offer, and what is not told is that much of this information was verbal and pertained to ritual.

Though Whare Ra withdrew from the Stella Matutina in 1931, no changes were made to its rituals (which were never watered down versions the English Temples used), but were the original Golden Dawn procedures. This was driven home to my wife and I when, through Jack Taylor's efforts, we were fortunate enough to meet a number of ex-Whare Ra Temple members, whose skill at Ritual could simply be described as astounding, even though they had little scholarship. This of course did not apply to all Temple members, but to a select few who held the main Officers positions for up to twenty years with barely any interruption. By this, I mean Officers who for the main part were continually reelected, during the latter part of Whare Ra's history.

We became the recipients of their expertise, and from this teaching gradually became aware of the existence of the six main Golden Dawn currents. One of the strange things we found out is that while each Temple Officer knew of each others respective positions, few if any, had any idea of what their counterparts were doing. With Taylor's influence however, we managed to gather this information collectively for operation in the Thoth Hermes Temple. Apparently, the snobbish structure of Whare Ra prevented this type of communication between Temple members, and few had any real idea of their fellow members real potential, other than of their direct seniors in charge of ritual.

Take the Neophyte Ritual again as an example. After the Hierophant activates the Astral Shells, they stay activated until the Hierophant breaks the etheric link, for it is he that activates the current of Osiris. When the Officers take their places on the floor of the Temple at the beginning of the ceremony, the activated Shells of the godforms then link with their physical auras. Because of the delicate nature of this linking (these Auric Shells are sometimes seen clairvoyantly as light green in colour), it must be done correctly on two levels: the first by the Hierophant, and the second by the Temple Officer. In the old Order, the Temple Officers were to hold low Outer Order Grades, but with the discoveries of those Adepti of Whare Ra (whose Temple Officers were almost always Inner Order), it's quite clear that all the Officers on the Temple floor should be Inner Order to correctly control the power and direct it. For they have to manipulate their own Sphere of Sensation and vibrate it to the rhythm of the ritual they are doing.

While the Hierophant of the Temple creates the Astral Shells before the ritual starts, this does not extend to the Astral Shells of the godforms on the Dais, (apart from his own Osiris Shell). These are, in fact, activated by the Officers on the Dais, with the Imperator linking with Nephthys current. Instead of sitting and observing the rituals, they in fact have a great deal of work to do which gives the Hierophant the much needed boost to the ceremony. They also control flow rates of power as well. Out of all these currents, the most important of all is the Thoth current; for without it the rituals become mere dramatic gestures. The Z-1 Document, prefaced by the General Exordium, is a fair indication of the powers and duties of Thoth.

The following paper was a Flying Rolls paper issued out in the Thoth Hermes Temple which also explains the function of the rituals from a Kabbalistic concept.

Flying Roll 37
KABBALISTIC SOUL AND AURA
ACTIVATION DURING RITUAL

By now most of you will be familiar with the three main principles of the Kabbalistic Soul (Neschamah, Ruach and Nephesch).

The importance of understanding this principle is because during ritual, the link of the three aspects of the Soul opens the gate to a tremendous source of energy. If we study how this energy can be acquired, we use the principles of the aura as a method of expanding this principle. The aura around the body is made up of images of the man, which start next to the skin, and can be seen extending 6 to 12 feet from the physical body. Some have grouped these images together in 7 stages, but the fact remains that they all emanate from the physical in shape, and can be attributed to the Nephesch.

The Ruach during ritual is the Astral Shell the Hierophant creates before the ritual begins, and which the Officers step into. (The method of doing this will be explained at higher grades). This is the accumulated unconscious energy of the Order which is drawn from the matrix and sent back when the ceremony is completed. When the Temple Officer silently meditates, he consciously links his aura with the Shell which opens up new channels of awareness within him.

The Neschamah is the divine spark brought about by the Ruach and Nephesch, linked with the Officer stretching forth his faculty of reason; all are joined as a unified force by the Hierophant who welds them together as he brings down the power of the Order which could be classed as the Neschamah. While this entire principle is inherited in us as living beings (with the Neschamah as our soul or disassociated state of awareness), we have in fact learned to extend this faculty via group ritual working.

As one advances through the ranks of the Order, the aura is impregnated with the vital forms of each element grade. This forces a link between your own aura and the Ruach of the Order. It is power which binds the two together in a positive manner, the link being stronger with each grade you undertake. This makes it easier each time for the power of the Neschamah to give the divine spark and bind to the Ruach, to come through during ceremony. It is not unusual, if this is done correctly, for the aura to light up, and /or images appear around the Officer and grade, but shows that the Nephesch, Ruach, and Neschamah, have linked together correctly. Generally imbalances in these ceremonies occur when the Ruach has blocked off the power of Neschamah, and in cases like these the onus is on the Hierophant or another Officer to bring them together.

At the close of the ceremony the Neschamah withdraws, and the Ruach unbinds, leaving the Nephesch revitalised and replenished. The Order aspect of the Kabbalistic Soul cannot function correctly unless these three phases in our own beings are operating. The joining point is when our own Ruach links with the Order created Ruach, which allows the energy to be passed through the Nephesch at a particular point.

CHAPTER 4

ENOCHIAN PRONUNCIATION

In the past there has been a lot of criticism about the Golden Dawn's Enochian pronunciation, based solely on two papers published by Regardie in his "Golden Dawn" publication. The first of these two paper is by Wynn Westcott who says:

> **In pronouncing the Names, take each letter separately. M is pronounced Em; N is pronounced En (also Nu, since in Hebrew the vowel following the equivalent letter Nun is "u"); A is Ah; P is Peh; S is Ess; D is Deh. NRFM is pronounced En-Ra-Ef-Em or En-Ar-Ef-Em. ZIZA is pronounced Zod-ee-zod-ah. ADRE is Ah-deh-reh. TAAASD is Teh-ah-ah-Ess-deh. AIAOAI is Ah-ee-ah-of-ah-ee. BDOPA is Beh-deh-of-peh-ah. BANAA is Beh-ah-en-ah-ah. BITOM is Beh-ee-to-eem or Beh-ee-teh-oo-em. NANTA is En-ah-en-tah. HCOMA is Heh-co-em-ah. EXARP is Eh-ex-ar-peh.**

The Mathers paper, to quote Dr. Laycock, "is essentially the same system, but with some idiosyncractic viewpoints." When Israel Regardie compiled his Enochian dictionary, he based his pronunciation guide on these two papers. Other occult writers have also concluded that this was the Golden Dawn method, but in fact this is an erroneous assumption. When Jack Taylor gave me my copy of *"The Concourse of Forces,"* I noticed on my printed copy (which was a Golden Dawn original) the two modes of pronunciation given; that is, both long and short vowels.

Unfortunately, this has never appeared on any of the published versions of *"The Concourse of Forces,"* but it clearly shows the two modes of pronunciation within the Order. What was taught at Whare Ra, by Felkin, was that the long vowel mode of pronunciation as advocated by Mathers and Westcott was only used when one wanted to emphasize a certain word or phrase. The other aspects of Enochian Invocation, that is the short vowel form, was used much the same way as any other type of invocation used. In order that there was no confusion between the two, the Order had an "Enochian Vocabulary" in which the pronunciation of each word is given, using the short vowel form. Some years ago I was given Dr. Felkin's copy (dated 1897) which, is a rare gem. A short prayer at the back of the book gave, and showed the use of, the two vowel forms.

Felkin taught that one could also make up their own invocations using the Enochian language (as Crowley did when he translated certain evocations of the Goetia into the Enochian tongue). Though the Enochian Vocabulary does not appear on any official Order papers for circulation, there were a number circulated privately. This was mainly due in part to the lack of interest in Enochiana by the Adepti, and the number of other Mathers documents circulated that were utilized by a select few (such as alchemical translations).

When I showed Felkin's Enochian Vocabulary to Regardie and told him of the Whare Ra mode of pronunciation, he admitted that if this was in operation at the Bristol Temple when he was there, it was never shown to him. He was not surprised, however, and said that the Chiefs of Bristol showed no inclination to Enochian work whatsoever.

Some years ago when I first started experimenting with the Enochian Calls, I found that in the astral, the Enochian Entities would return calls of their own. Some of the Whare Ra Adepti who did use the Calls also told me that this was not unusual, though the tone I received back was entirely different to the one I uttered. Firstly it was flat; roughly in the scale of "C," and there was very little pause between words, with it being said in the short vowel form. The whole thing sounded to me like an Indian Mantram effect. I mention this in case some of the readers may have had a similar experience.

The following vocabulary of the Golden Dawn is include for those who wish to experiment with the Enochian Calls.

THE MAGICAL LANGUAGE: "A VOCABULARY"

FINEM RESPICE
June 19, 1897

A

Abiding *(their)*	Kâfăfam
According to *(in accordance with)*	
Add	Vanmel
Admiration	Jirèsam
Are	Cahis
Are *(and are not)*	I cahisjè
Age, an Aeon	Min
All things	Tofajilo
Always	Paid
Amongst *(ye)*	Aáî
Amongst us	Aáiomé
And	od (sometimes **x**, rarely **z·**)
All powerful *(the)*	Ia-I-don
Anger	Vaunupeh
Another	Ka

Appareled *(are)*	Zodonak
Appear	Zodamran
Apply *(yourself to us)*	Im´-uȧ-mar
are *(see above)*	
Arise	Torzodu
Ark	Erem
Ark *(of knowledge)*	Iadanah
Art *(thou)*	Ieh
As	Ta

B

Balance	Piâpé
Barren Stone	Oreri
Beautiful	Vaurebsa
Beauty	Turèbìs
Beasts *(of the field)*	Lenithmoug
Beginning	Tpamè. Taoda, Faoda, Iadof
Beginning	Acro-odzodi
Become *(thus are ye become)*	Naomi
Be *(it shall)*	Tariam
Bed	Tainta
Beneath *(ye)*	Orocaha
Before *(in front of)*	Asapta
Be *(thou)*	Bolap
Be *(that it may be)*	Noalaun
Because	Bajlen
Bindeth *(together)*	Comemahe
Bitter sting	Jiroseb
Blood *(of)*	Kauila

Bring down	Darixor, Daribo
Breath *(the living)*	Jijipah
Bring forth	Yolacam
Bringing forth	Yolaki
Brother	È-si-asacah
Bucker	Lolpis
Building *(a)*	Taurof
Buildings	Kat-bèl
Branches	Iisonon
Brightness	Lukiftias
Burn *(to)*	Ialpou
Burning	I-al: Olpiret

C or K

Called *(is)*	Ivanmed
Cast *(down)*	Adarepau
Caves *(as the)*	Tabèjèsa or Tabjes
Centre	Oǔoăreś, Elzodape
Chamber	Qojè
Circle	Komselahe
Comfort *(of)*	Belioret, Beliorab
Comfort *(our)*	Beliores
Comfort	Beliores
Comfort *(visit with)*	Fa-beliahed
Comfort	Pi-beliarè
Come ye, come away	Nilsa
Comefort *(thou shalt)*	B´liorax
Comeforter *(in our)*	Bijliad

Comeforter *(continued)*	Be-lior
Confound	Ovaukaho, Vaunkalu
Conquest	Zoailodarepe
Contents *(of mine)*	Qo-Kó-Lasab
Continuance	Miamè
Course	Zodare
Courses	Elauzodape
Covered	Etahamezod
Covenant	Sibesi
Creation	Qaä
Creation *(in our)*	Qoaaou
Creation *(your)*	Qoaän
Creator *(the)*	Qoál
Creatures	Hámi
Cried with a loud voice	Bahalâ
Creature *(no)*	Toltorèm
Creature *(no one)*	Torètorìum
Creatures *(all)*	Tolalianiè
Crown	Mómaŏ
Cups	Talabo
Curse	Anima

D

Darkness *(with)*	Oresâ
Darts *(fiery)*	Malâpereji
Day	Basajinu
Death	Teloahe
Death *(of)*	Teloahe

# THE SECRET INNER ORDER RITUALS OF THE GOLDEN DAWN

Defaced *(lettered)*	To midĝi
Delivered *(i.e. gave)*	Zodouurenusâpi
Deliverers *(pleasant)*	Obelisonuji
Depth *(in the)*	Pi-Adâpehe
Descend *(ye)*	Vânijilaji
Destroy	Quasâbè
Diamonds	Cubiŝadăo
Differ *(let them)*	Dilâ Toâmo
Diminish	Pered Zodarè
Dispose *(to)*	Poilâpè
Division	Yirèpoilâ
Down *(bring)*	Dariloa
Dragon *(the)*	Vouińa
Dryness *(with)*	Oresâcouè
Drunken	Oresâba, Oresaha
Dwell	Perafa
Dwelling place *(the)*	Fabrèjita
Dwelling place *(their)*	Farejita
Dwelling *(living)*	Pa-ra-dial

E

Eagle	Vabèzodirè
Earth *(the)*	Caosâji, Caosaga
Earth *(of the)*	Caosâjo
Earth *(for the)*	Caosâji
Earth *(than the)*	Caosaginu
Earthquakes	Gizodyazod
East *(the)*	Ra-asa
East (into the)	Ra-asy

Echoing	Matorib
Empty	Afâfa
Ends	Vâlâsâ
End (cannot be)	Latpausisâ
Entered	Zodímǔ, Nomiji
Everliving (the)	Ioiada
Everyone of ye	Vomèsaȓgi
Eyes	Ooaoua, Ooanoan
Exalted (in power)	Elanusâhè
Except	Mè

F

Face	Adoiánn
Fall	Lonncaho
Fall (such as)	Coȓsâta Dobilza
Fallen	Vimè
Faith	Gono
Feet (their)	eLusâda
Feet (with)	eLusâdanu
Feet (your)	eLusâda
Feet (my)	ELasâdi
Fire	Perèjì
Fires of life	Malâ Pireji
Fire of first glory	Jla Pire Gah'
Fire of	Perejel
Fiery darts	Malapèrèji
Firmament (the)	Callzod

Firmament of the waters	Oila-zodinu
First	El-o, Ela, El
Flame	Vêpè, Pereta
Flames *(the burning)*	Iala-pėrėjî
Flames *(of the first)*	El Iala Pèritâ
Flames *(of the second)*	Viv Iala Pèritâ
Flames *(of the third)*	Da Iala Pèritâ
Flaming *(adj.)*	Iala Porè
Flew *(they)*	Zodiláďarè
Flourish *(they)*	Ka-ca-comè
Flowers	Elorèsá, Bajilé
For *(i.e. because)*	Elapè
Forget *(let them)*	Bamèaâ
Fourth angle *(the)*	Sa Diú
Framed *(I have)*	I-zoda-zaz
Friendly *(be ye)*	Zod Ōrèjè
Frown *(They Frown not)*	VâKimè
Furnishing	Tóŏatâ
Fury	Voonpèhé
Fury	Noŕóini Bajihié

G

Garland	Obèloka
Garments *(your)*	Qäa, obolshi
Garnished	Jinouupè
Gathering *(of)*	Alâdi
Gather *(these gather)*	Alâdonu
Giving *(unto them)*	Dâlagarè

Giving	Daluga
Given *(is given)*	Idâlugamè
Girdles *(your)*	Ataraahe
Glory *(ing)*	Basâda, Bufâdâ
Glory *(that they)*	Busadirè
God	Iadâ, Madâ
God *(of god)*	Oïadâ
Going before	Tasatatzâ
Govern *(to)*	Kaba
Government *(for the)*	Netáaïbé
Government *(ing)*	Anétabè
Governments *(of your)*	De Genátáăbe
Govern *(govern ye)*	Tabaoui
Governed *(let be g.)*	Tabaorèdâ
Governor *(the)*	Tabaäm
Great	Darilâpa, Darisâpa
Great name *(the)*	Mouasâci
Greater	Drilâpi
Groaned aloud *(if)*	Holâdo
Guard *(a)*	Bèranñsâji

H

Hands	Zo-oel, Zodienn
Hands *(mine own)*	Ozodienu
Hands *(on whose)*	Azodienu

THE SECRET INNER ORDER RITUALS OF THE GOLDEN DAWN 131

Hands *(in the palms of)*	Ta Noblèlohè Zodienu
Happy is he	Vâlâkińinu
Harboured *(are h.)*	Bèlanusâ
Harlot *(of)*	A-babalonudâ
Harvest	Azodiájiere
Hearken	Toáterè
Heart	Monomes
Hearken at once	Solâ-Bi-Enu
Heads *(their)*	Dazodi sâ Ózodól
Heavens	Pè Ripèsol, Peripèsal Za
Heavens of ye	Madrüatzâ, Madriatzâ
Heavens *(the third)*	Madâriatzâ, Pi-Ripèsonn
Heavens *(the lower)*	Oádâriatzâ
Her *(of her)*	Tilabè
Her	Tiobèlâ
Herein	Emèna
Highest *(of all)*	Tzodizodope, Izizopè
Highest *(God the)*	IAIDA
Him, His	Totza
"Him that is, was and shall be crowned."	Iadaoiasamomare
Holy ones *(the)*	Pirè
Honour *(the seal of)*	Emtajisa, Iaiádiza
Honour *(the)*	Mosâ Pelèhè
House	Salâmann, Isalâmame
Hundred *(all)*	Vóhimè
Hyacinth pillars	Nazâvabébè

I

I	Oel
I am	Zodirèdo
In	Qo, I, Do, Ta, OO
Increase *(noun)*	Pilâdâ
Increase the thunders of:	Ananags
Iniquity	Madâridâ
Is	I
Is *(which is)*	Dasa I
Is not *(as)*	Tage
Intent	Fafenn

J

Jaws *(in the depth of my)*	Pi-ádâpáhè
Joy	Mozod
Judgment	Zodizirasâ
Just *(the)*	Oïada
Just *(this)*	Balifâ
Justice *(of)*	Balâtâ
Justice *(his)*	Bálâtánn
"Justice, extreme or fury"	Balatimè

K

Kingdoms	Elouu-dohè
Knowledge *(the use defiled)*	Iadâ nămadâ
Knowledge *(the ark of)*	Iadâ Nahè
Known *(let her be known)*	Izomátzipé

L

Laid up	Maäsi
Lamentation *(of)*	Cŏpèhánn
Lamp *(living or everburning)*	Húbăré, Hubăro
Lanterns	Hubãis
Law *(I make a law)*	Hohorála
Let there be	Cahèristeosa
Lift up	Goholoré
Lift up your voices	Farèzodamè
Likeness *(in our)*	Azíăzōrè
Liveth for ever	Apĭla
Liveth *(he that)*	Jadăpila
Lord *(the)*	Enayo
Looking with gladness	Dorèpèhala

M

Made *(I)*	E-óelâ
Manifold Winds *(the)*	Ozodonugouu
Many *(how many)*	Irèjíla
Marble	Fidiai
Marrow *(of the)*	Târanann
Measure *(I)*	Holâ-gi
Measured *(are)*	Holâgo
Men	Olâlore
Men *(the row of)*	Nonè-mo-lapèvlarè
Mercy *(of)*	Rita
Mercies *(his)*	Iehúsozod
Midst *(in the)*	Notahoa, Zodomèdâ

Midday, the first.	Bazodmelo
Mighty	Mi-Ká-olâzod
Mighty sounds	Kapaho, Midali
Might (be)	O-mi-ca-ol-zod
Mightier	Micalâpè
Mind (in the)	Maninn
Milestones	Aniny
Minister	Qouodi
Moon (the)	Giraa
Moreover	Pilahè
Moss	Momè
Mouth (the)	Butâmonn
Mouths (from their)	Butâmuoi
Move	Zod'âcárè
Move ye (I)	Zodacamè
Mysteries	Kikalè, Kikalèsâ

N

Name (in the)	Do-o-i-apè, Do-O-a-ipè
Name (his)	Do-O-a-inn
Name (whose)	Ioba-Dooain
Names (their)	Omaóas
Nest	Viròqo
Nine	EM
No place	Ripirè
None	Aji
Not (is not)	Je
North (in the)	Lucalâ

Numbers	Corèmèfa
Numbers	Sa-ga-cor
Number of times	Capimaonn
Numbered	Corèmèpè, Cormpt
Numbered *(hath)*	Corèmèpo

O

Oak	Paobè
Obedience	Adâna
Obey	Darèbèsâ
Olives in the Olive Mount.	a-a-misâ Adaroeabè
One	Elâ
One *(the all one)*	Ilâ
O Thou	Iâsâ
Outward	Fifalâzod
Over	Voresa
Over Ye	Vorèsaji
O Ye	Nomki

P

Palace, Palaces	Poamala
Palm *(of the hand)*	Nobèlohè
Partakers	Pèlápèli
Parts *(of her)*	Saamirè
Pillars, Hyacinth	Na-zodambèbè
Pillars of gladness	Na-Zodaretahe
Placed *(I)*	Aăla
Placed *(I have)*	O'ăla

Planted *(he Hath)*	Harèji
Pleasure	Qasahi
Pleasant	Obelisonnji
Poison	Faboann
Power *(in)*	Elonnsahi, Mickalazōdo
Power	Elonnsa
Power *(my)*	Na-e-el
Power *(exalted in)*	Elannsâhè
Powers *(their)*	Elonnsahinn
Pomp in	Auăuolsa
Powerful	Ia-i-donn
Pouring down	Pannpire
Power *(in presence of)*	Gi-mi-caelzodo
Power *(of understanding)*	Karinn, Vimikal, Zodoma
Praise	E-Karim
Praise *(that ye may)*	Resata-el
Praises *(singing)*	Oé-Karĭmu
Prepared *(I have)*	Abèramèji
Prepared *(are)*	Abèramiji
Promise	Isàro, Aisâro
Provided *(he)*	Abràasâsa
Providence	Varèryì

R

Reasoning creatures	Korèdâziz
Receivers	Eda Naia
Rejoiceth *(he)*	Kahirèlann
Remain	Pa-Aŏtza
Remembrance	Papènor'

Reign *(I)*	Sonnfa
Reigneth *(which)*	Bojira
Repent *(I)*	Moóoabe
Requireth *(it or he)*	Uniji
Rest not	Pajeipé
Reveal, revealest	Odo
Righteous *(the)*	Samuelâji
Righteousness *(the divine)*	Baconibe
Righteous *(of)*	Piamoel, Balatohé
Rich	Iasâ ^
Rise	Torzodu
Rise *(Shall)*	Torzoduel
Robe	Mabezoda
Rock	Patâranutza
Rod	Cabé
Run *(let it)*	Parèmèji

S

Saith *(he)*	Gohoo
Salt *(of)*	Baliè
Same *(the)*	Elela
Save *(example)*	O, Me, Ca, Repè
Say *(I)*	Gohoosa
Say *(we)*	Gohia
Saying	Gohola
Said *(it is)*	Gohulim
Said *(they have)*	Gohonn
Saith the first	Gohè-ela
Scorpious	Siatarisa, Tahilann

Seas	Zodumibi
Seats *(thrones)*	Tahila, Otahila
Season	Nimèbè
Second	Vi-Vâ
Second Angel *(the)*	Vi-Va-Di-Vâ
Second Beginning of things	Karŏ-ŏ-dâzi
Secret Wisdom *(the)*	Anánaelâ
Secrets of truth	Laiádâ ^
See *(shall not)*	Ipurann
Seer	Varelâré
Separatest *(thou)*	Taliobè
Servant	Noco
Servant *(his)*	No-Quoda
Servants	Quonn
Serve *(let it serve them)*	Boöapisâ
Serve *(let them serve ye)*	Aboäperi
Shall be	Tariann
Shineth *(it)*	So-bŏlo
Sickles *(sharp)*	Pu-îmè
Sing Praises	Oekârimi
Sink	Karèbáfâ
Sin	Doalimè
Sit	Târnutâ
Six	Nórĭzod
Sleep	Beréda
Skirts	Vaualahe
Spake	Kameliatza
Sons	Norè

Sons *(of ye sons)*	Noroni
Song of honour	La-Iá-Hé
Sorrow (of)	Tibibèpè
Sounds of Mighty	Salàhè, Nidáli
South	Babájè
Spake *(he)*	Camèlialz`á
Spirits (the)	Gahè
Stand	Biáhè
Stars	Aôivéaé
Stewards	Balâzodarèji
Stone *(the barren)*	Orèri
Stooping Dragon *(the)*	Abai´uouinn
Sting	Jirosâbe
Stranger	Gosaä
Strength *(our)*	Vâmèpèlífâ
Strong *(make me)*	Ozazamè
Strong *(wax or become)*	Vâjéji, Va-jé-ji
Stronger	Ji ûi
Successively	Kapè-mi-áli
Stir up	Lârinuji, Zodixâlay
Such	Córèsa
Such (suits)	Córèsi
Sulphur	Sálâbèrozâ
Sun	Rosè
Surges	Mòliṅ
Sware *(ye did)*	Zodnnriza
Sworn *(he hatch)*	Surèzasa
Sword	Nozodpèsadâ
Swords *(of ye)*	Napeâi
Swords	Napêta

T

Talked *(I have T. of ye)*	Be-Ri-Ta
Temple	Siâionn
Terror *(unto thee)*	Kiâisi
That *(which)*	Dasa
Their	No
Therefore	Eka
These	Vaunesâ, Vannalâ
Third	Dau
Third angle	Da-i-be
3rd Heaven	Pi-Ripson
Thorns	Euannba
Thoughts *(his)*	Anňgelaridá
Thou	Ilâsâ
Thousand	Eorèsâ, Matâbâ
Through thrusting fire	Matâpèrèji
Thunders	Konnsâtâ
Thunders *(to increase)*	Auanago
Thunders *(of judgement)*	Koraxo
Thus all ye became	
Times	Kothasâ
Time *(true ages of)*	Homila
Torment	Mire
Towers	Es-I-Ma-dea
Train (our)	Fafeen
Treasure	Limelila
Triumpheth	Homètohè
Truth	Yöoano
Truth *(the secrets of)*	Laíadâ
True worship	Hoâtahè

U

Under ye	Orokahè
Understanding *(that)*	Dasomè
Understanding	Omèpè
Understanding *(a power U.)*	Jimicalâzodoma
Unspeakable	Adâpehaheta
Until	Kâkarèji
Unto *(us)*	Pujo

V

Variety	Damèpèlozod
Vessels	Zodizoddope
Vestures *(my)*	Zodimèzod
Vex *(let them v.)*	Dodâpal
Vexation	Dodâsihè
Vexed	Dodârèmèni
Visit	Fa
Visit us	Epa
Voice	BIANU
Virgins	Para di zod
Voice	Sol-pefâhé bunn
Voices *(yours)*	Bia
Voices *(ye lift up your v.)*	Faresodniè
Voices of wonder	Salâdâ
Vials	Efafije
Vomit out	Otzetza

W

Walkest *(thou)*	Imîsi
Water *(to)*	Zodlida
Water *(firmament of)*	Pila zodinu

Wax strong	Vâujeji
Wedding	Paralleda
West	Bolânn
While *(one w.)*	El Ka Pimas
Where in	Quiinn
Who	Daśa
Whom	Kasarèma, Sobamè
Whom *(unto)*	Kasaremè
Whome	Kasarèmieji
Whome *(under)*	Kaseremi
Widow	Riore
Windows	Kouio
Winds	Zodougou
Winds *(the many fold w.)*	Ozodoùuguù
Wings	Vâ pa ahe
Widsom *(the secret)*	Anánaelá
Woe	Ohis
Work of man	Konisâbèra
Workmen	Kanalâ
Work wonders *(that may)*	Uaula zodirèmn
Works *(whose)*	Sobè lia afake
Worshippers	Hoatáhè
Wrath	Vênupèhì
Wrath *(the firmament of)*	Kaelzod

Y

You *(unto you)*	Nounca
Yourselves	Amirann

CHAPTER 5

THE 6=5 and 7=4 RITUALS OF THE STELLA MATUTINA OF THE R.R. et A.C.

According to tradition, these rituals were written through the trance mediumship of the Felkins with the Astral Masters of the Third Order. The general opinion at Whare Ra was that the 6=5 Grade is an incredibly beautiful ceremony to experience. It is here that the hidden doorway of the Mars Wall is revealed, and the Shekinah enters the Vault, with black veil and lamp. To the Postulant, it appears as if the lamp is floating in mid-air. This is the first of the rituals where the Shekinah takes over the astral body of the Adept, and lifts it out of the Vault. It then takes it to meet the various forms. In my own case, and others within both the Whare Ra and Thoth Hermes Temples, this is exactly what happens. For in the next two ceremonies, a great deal occurs on the astral level.

The outline of the 6=5 Ceremony is like that of the 6th Masonic degree; a natural progression from the 5=6 which is also likened to a Masonic ritual in basic essence. At the 6=5 Grade, the costumes of the Officers undergo a dramatic change. The Egyptian headdress is now discarded for a small colored square cloth with colored rope wound around the top to keep it in place. Included after the 6=5 Ritual are some notes I made a few years ago as a part of my 6=5 thesis, and I have included here as a matter of interest.

The 7=4 Ceremony uses the two outer rooms of the Vault, and the notes included with the ritual were, I presume, written by Felkin, as they were given to me by Taylor after going through this Grade Ceremony.

The final ritual is called "Transmission of the Etheric Link," and was only given out to a few at Whare Ra. It's purpose was to transmit the link of the Order in its fullest capacity to the Adept. This was only given out at 7=4 Level and is not a substitute for any Grade Ceremony, but in fact seals off the Link in the Adept's Aura. Why this was given out in the 7=4 Grade and not 8=3 or 9=2 Levels is not clear. It is slightly complicated but in essence is as follows. During Felkins reign on the Temples, the 8=3 and 9=2 Grades were left for those who had made contact with the Third Order. However, when Felkin gave out these grades to the Chiefs of the other British Temples who had not made this contact, the Chiefs of said Temples treated these two higher grades as nothing more than Temple Grades, given out to those who had devoted a lifetime of effort to the Order. I was told this by a former Chief of Whare Ra, Bethany Jones when I quizzed her about those grades and their significance.

Mrs. Felkin told Jack Taylor that the 7=4 Grade was the last of the physical grades, and not to bother with the other ones. The Etheric Link brought in at this level seals the aura of the Adept, and theoretically gives him the highest level of energy the Order has to offer. No one really believed that those of 8=3 or 9=2 Grades were Adepts beyond the physical. This stemmed over from the old Golden Dawn Temples.

One could say that the bottom line of the Babe of the Abyss, 8=3 and 9=2 Grades is that they were temple Grades only, their power base was the supplementation of what the rituals included as a teaching mechanism included and core components of structures were needed to keep them separate but also allow for the flow pattern of energy to make its presence known by opening up additional layers to be examined. Since the first edition of the book I have done a complete 180 degree turn, over a twenty year period, on my viewpoint on the levels above 7=4 as my understanding of the Golden Dawn system evolved. These higher grades above the 7=4 are mere reflections of what is contained within them and how the adept develops in their current.

THE 6=5 RITUAL

SHEKINAH or MATRONA: rose-coloured tunic, long black veil, alabaster lamp with oil, spray of acacia.

CHIEF ADEPT: KING OF SALEM: blue and purple nemyss and robe, ankh, winged sphere wand and lamen.

SECOND ADEPT: EXCELLENT PRINCE OF THE HORIZON: red and orange nemyss and robe, ankh, phoenix wand and lamen.

POSTULANT: *(in 1st point)* black cowl *(in 2nd point)* purple cloak, red slippers.

THIRD ADEPT: NOBEL LORD OF EVENTIDE: yellow and rose robe and nemyss, ankh, lotus wand and lamen.

THE VAULT is entirely draped in red. The pastos in black stands uncovered, with the head to the north. Pedestal at the head. Light veiled.

WHARE RA VAULT PLAN

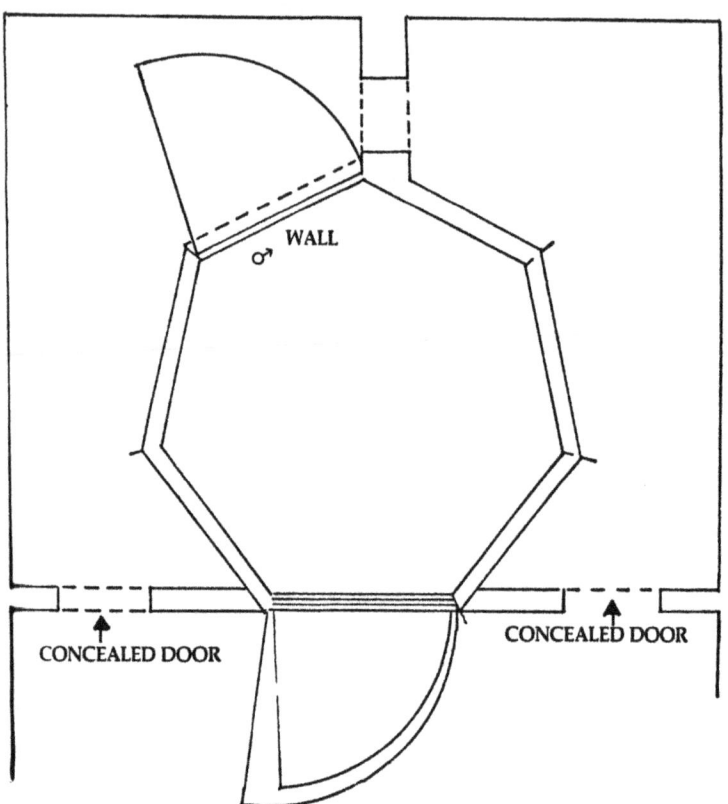

In PORTAL: two pillars, red ankh holding brazier at south. Blue tat holding bowl of water at north. Outer side of the vault door covered with blue curtain on which is orange Sol on cross. Strip of emerald-green cloth up the centre of the floor. White and gold altar divided middle. Thirty-three lights, 2 extinguishers.

The three Adepti sit in triangle facing the vault. The Postulant must receive full instructions as to silence, knocks and gestures beforehand. Bell *(used in opening, location, who rings it not mentioned)*, candle for Chief Adept to take into vault. Censer. Tarot keys of Justice and the Hanged Man for 2nd point. Strip of linen to bind Postulant in 2nd point. Hierophant's lamen for 1st point. Scales with heart and feather for second point. Preparation of the "Light" by Shekinah: She pours the olive oil into the alabaster lamp and says: *"The oil is the life of the Tree, let the Tree give its life."* She mingles her blood with the oil and says: *"The blood is the life of the man, let the man give his life."* As she kindles the light in the oil, she says: *"The light is the life of the world, let all the living rejoice."*

OPENING

Ch. Ad.: rises ! 2nd Adept: !! 3rd Adept !!!
Ch. Ad.: Avete Fratres et Sorores all rise
Ch. Ad. + 2nd Ad.: in unison Benedictus Dominus Deus Noster.
All present, led by **3rd Ad.:** Que dedit nobis Hoc Signum.
All touch Rose Cross on breast
Ch. Ad.: Very honoured Adepti Majores, assist me to open the Vault of the Adepti in the exalted grade of Geburah.
Ch. Ad.: Excellent Prince of the Horizon, see that all present have been admitted to the mystery.
2nd Ad.: Very Honoured Fratres et Sorores, give the sign. Done.
Ch. Ad.: Noble Lord of Eventide, what is the word?
3rd Ad.: Elohim Gibor.
Ch. Ad.: Grant us thy strength, oh Lord! Excellent Prince of the Horizon, what is the mystic number formed therefrom?
2nd Ad.: The number is 20.
Ch. Ad.: Noble Lord of Eventide, what is the signification thereof?

3rd Ad.: It is the union of the Enochian tablets and the Kerubic emblems.
Ch. Ad.: The Lord is my strength and my song.
2nd Ad.: He is also become by salvation.
Ch. Ad.: In the strength of Elohim Gibor, let us with tranquil minds and recollected hearts enter into the Valley of the Shadow.
2nd Ad.: Thou wilt keep him in perfect peace whose mind is stayed on thee.
3rd Ad.: The Night cometh and also the day; if ye will return, return ye. Turn down the light in the vault.
Ch. Ad. & 2nd Ad.: open the door of the vault and enter.
Ch. Ad.: passes to east and takes candle.
2nd Ad.: remains at west.
3rd Ad.: remains without.
One bell ring.
Ch. Ad.: Oh death, where is thy sting?
2nd Ad.: Oh grave, where is thy victory?
Ch. Ad. & 2nd Ad.: Thanks be to God which gives us the victory!
They place their wands with the ends resting within the pastos and raise their ankhs joining them above wands.
Ch. Ad.: Say then, my brother, what is the emblem which we raise above the grave?
2nd Ad.: It is the symbol of life; the union of the girdle of the Great Mother with the Tau cross of death; it is the emblem of that eternal life of spirit which the Divine Ones pour forth among men, delivering him from the body of Death.
Ch. Ad.: Verily thou hast answered well, my brother. Let us then entreat the Great Mother thus to raise us all from the death of the soul to life in the spirit.

They turn to the north east, still keeping their wands in the pastos but separating their ankhs, which they raise in invocation. They sink on one knee. **3rd Ad.** *also kneels and rises without ankh.*

Ch. Ad.: Mother of life, hidden home of the Fire of the Spirit, grant to us thy life. Mother of all, Matrona, we would be even as the burning bush, which was not consumed–a sign to those who may have eyes to see. Star of the Sea, in thy hands is the lamp of understanding, show us, if for an instant, a ray of that Light Divine. Rose of the world, vouchsafe to us breath of thine ineffable fragrance. Tower of ivory, enclose us in thy protecting purity. Give us, we beseech thee, this day and hour, thine aid in the high purpose for which we are here assembled. Strengthen the Postulant, who seeketh enlightenment through the gates of darkness; that passing through the valley of bitterness, he may therein find the Wells of Living Water. Reflect upon his soul those visions of the Spirit which will awaken the understanding and beckon us to the Pisgah Heights of Holiness. There may he find the Pearl of Great Price which is the Lodestone of the Wise. SHEKINAH!

2nd Ad.: Shekinah!
3rd Ad.: Shekinah!
All 3 Adepti: Shekinah!
3rd Ad.: turns up the light in the vault.

The vault, which was in darkness at first, gradually becomes lighter, revealing the figure of Shekinah, holding a lamp under her veil. At the last word she holds forth the lamp in silence, letting the light shine on the Adepti in turn. They bow their heads a moment. Shekinah withdraws silently. The Adepti rise and quit the vault in silence.

POINT ONE

Vault light out. Vault door is closed. Adepti seated in triangle. Postulant has been previously instructed in knocks, etc. He is robed in white, with black cord round waist, black cowl overhead, black slippers. He carries Hierophant's lamen. **3rd Ad.** *goes out and sees that he is duly prepared, then returns, leaving door slightly ajar. Postulant knocks once, hesitatingly. Inside a bell sounds twice.*

2nd Ad.: The hour of night approaches; the shades of evening close in; he who hath wandered far, travelling through the heat and burden of the day, seeketh rest.
Ch. Ad.: Let us then redeem the time. Excellent Prince of the Horizon, where is the place of rest?
2nd Ad.: East of the Sun and west of the Moon. *(Postulant knocks more firmly)* Rest after toil doth greatly please.
Ch. Ad.: How then hath he who seeketh for entrance prepared for that rest?
2nd Ad.: By a faithful obedience to the rules of our order; by that bodily purification which reflects the purity for which we strive; by the observation of abstinence and silence for a period of 20 hours; in token whereof we impose upon him the final test before admitting him within the portal.
He turns to **3rd Ad.** and says: Noble Lord of Eventide, before admitting the Postulant ascertain that his pledge is duly maintained. *Postulant knocks thrice urgently.*
3rd Ad.: opens door but bars the way saying: By what right seekest thou entrance to these sacred precincts?
Postulant in silence offers Heiro's lamen.
3rd Ad.: takes the lamen and stands aside to let Postulant in and then the **3rd Ad.** says: Merciful King of Salem, I have

tested the Postulant and silence is maintained.
Three bells sound. Postulant to the end of the carpet.
3rd Ad.: moves Postulant forward a few paces at each. "Who then is it?" until at the last "what then is this?" They are at the top of the steps facing the door of Vault.
Ch. Ad.: The hour cometh and even now is when the Son of Man shall appear. Art thou therefore prepared to discard the vestments of the flesh, that the soul unfettered may go forth to meet Him in the Air?
Postulant gives Sign of Osiris Slain. **2nd Ad.** *removes the black cowl standing behind Postulant.* **Ch. Ad.** & **2nd Ad.** *rise and turn towards him.* **Ch. Ad.** *raises wand and ankh on high.*
Ch. Ad.: Oh ye Divine Ones, who are in the presence of the supreme, grant me your arms, for I am he who shall come into being among you.
3rd Ad.: Who, then, is this?
2nd Ad.: I am the Divine Soul which dwelleth in the Seven Spheres.
3rd Ad.: Who, then, is this?
2nd Ad.: I am he who is not driven back among the Gods.
3rd Ad.: Who, then, is this?
2nd Ad.. I am yesterday; I know tomorrow.
Ch. Ad.: Yesterday is Osiris and tomorrow is Ra; I am the Only One, the Ruler of That Which is Made. Who, then, is this?
2nd Ad.: I am the Phoenix, the Living Present, arising from the ashes of the dead past; I am the Keeper of the Volume of the Book of Things which shall Be. Eternity is the Day and Everlastingness is the Night.
3rd Ad.: Who, then, is this?
2nd Ad.: I am Thooth, the scribe of the Holy Offerings; I am

he who riseth in his place, who cometh into the Holy City. I have made an end of my shortcomings and I have put away my faults.

3rd Ad.: *loosens cord from postulant's waist.*

3rd Ad.: What, then, is this?

2nd Ad.: It is the loosening in the corruptible in the body of Osiris, victorious before all the Gods; all his faults are driven out; it is the purification of Osiris on the day of his birth.

Ch. Ad.: I pass over the way; I know the Head of the Pool of Truth, even the Pool of Siloam, which is the Pool of Healing.

3rd Ad.: What, then, is this? *He points to door of vault.*

Ch. Ad.: It is the Northern Gate of the Underworld, even the Door of the Tomb whereon thou mayest behold the Sun in his Nadir, crucified between the Pillars of the Tree of Life. *All face east.*

Ch. Ad.: Homage unto Thee, oh Thou Lord of Light and Truth, oh Sovereign Prince who doest away with sin. Destroy Thou the faults that are within me, that with a clean heart I may approach when Thou dost say "Come therefore hither."

A pause. **Ch. Ad.** *turns to Postulant, who has been lead slowly forward during the forthgoing and now stands close to the door of the Vault.*

Already, Frater ***, a triple obligation rests upon thy soul; in Malkuth were thy feet bound, that they might keep in the Path of Judgment and Equity; on the Path of the Arrow thy loins were girt by the bonds of purity and self-restraint; in Tiphareth was thy heart bound by the threefold cord of love, service and sacrifice. Keep, therefore, the commandments of the Lord; bind them about thy neck; when thou goest they shall lead thee; when thou sleepest they shall keep thee; when thou wakest they shall talk with thee. Art thou then prepared having thus bound thy body with the spoken word, so now to bind thy soul with the silence from which thou art not yet loosed? If thou dost with thy mind assent, signify the same with the Sign of Light.

Postulant makes LVX signs in silence; **2nd Ad.** & **3rd Ad.** *place him back against door of Vault with arms outstretched, supporting arms.*

Ch. Ad.: He that findeth his soul shall loose it; and he that loseth his soul for My sake shall find it.

2nd Ad.: He that taketh not his Cross and followeth after Me, is not worthy of Me.

Four bells sound.

THE OBLIGATION

Ch. Ad. *recites the words and at the end of each clause the Postulant bows his head in silence.*

> 1. I, Frater ***, Associate Adeptus Minor of the 5 = 6 grade of the ancient Rosicrucian Fraternity of the Rose of Ruby and the Cross of Gold, standing here before the door of the Vault of the Adepti, do solemnly affirm and testify to the faith which I hold in my heart in those Greater Mysteries, to which the Lesser Mysteries are the door; I believe that they are implanted within the soul in silence and that through the Veils of Silence only can they be beheld. Standing thus in the sign of Osiris slain, with all sincerity and singleness of heart, do I affirm that I will ever maintain the most perfect silence in respect thereof. I promise that I will never reveal them to the profane, nor will I hint of them to those in the order who are below the rank of Theorici Adepti Majores.

2. I will henceforth endeavour to close my ears to the call of the evil and impure, whether around me or in my own heart, being well assured that he who gazes upon evil things or listens to the lure thereof–save only with the firm intention and will to stem its progress and transmute its power into the good, the true and the beautiful–can but increase that evil. As it is written, "Who is blind but my servant, or deaf as my messenger, whom I have sent."

3. Also will I be blind to the sins and weakness of others, save only when it is my high privilege to aid and raise those who seek for help. And may I be granted true humility and charity of spirit for such work.

4. I will henceforth pray continually that my own footsteps may not stumble, nor stray from that straight and narrow path of which it is said "few there be that find it." May I be guided therein by the Word, which is a lamp to those who seek; that laying aside every weight I may reach forth to that which is before us.

5. And finally, I will remember that the attainment of spiritual vision, or striving therefore, does in no wise lessen, but increases my obligations on the material plane; and in token thereof I will earnestly seek to live a pure and honourable life, to comfort those who mourn, to bind up the broken hearted, to proclaim liberty to the captives and the opening of prison to those who are bound and to bring Light to those who sit in darkness. And may Elohim Gibor give me strength to fulfil this vow.

3rd Ad. *brings censor to* **Ch. Ad.** *who censes Postulant in the form of a pentagram. Head, right foot, left hand, left right hand and up to head again.* **2nd Ad.** & **3rd Ad.** *lead him from the portal in science.*

End of first part.

POINT TWO

CANDLE ARRANGEMENT:

One-White

	(i)	(iii)	(ii)		(iv)	(v)	(i)	
One	Two	Four	Four		One	Four	Two	One
Blue	Brown	Green	Red		Red	Green	Brown	Blue
			(vi)	(v)	(vi)			
			Three	Seven	Three			
			Yellow	Violet	Yellow			

The Roman numbers are the ordering of extinguishing. Three are left lit.

The white altar is placed midway between the entrance and the door to the Vault. Upon it are arranged the coloured candles, unlit. West of this is an aisle supporting the Tarot keys of Justice and the Hanged Man, concealing the candles from the Postulant. **Ch. Ad.** & **2nd Ad.** *are seated on either side of the altar: the door of the vault is open.* **3rd Ad.** *remains in the west. Postulant now has bare feet except, for scarlet slippers and a purple cloak is thrown around him. The admission badge is a pair of scales with a heart in one scale and a feather on the other. 3rd adept goes to fetch the Postulant: As they enter, 5 bells sound.* **3rd Ad.** *puts aside the scales.*

Ch.Ad.: Who is this, who cometh from Edom with dyed garments from Bozrah?

2nd Ad.: I have trodden the winepress alone and of all the people there was none with me; and I looked and there was none to help and I wondered why there was none to uphold.

Ch. Ad.: It is good that a man should both hope and quietly wait for the salvation of the Lord, for he will not cast off for ever, for though he cause grief, yet he will have compassion according to the multitude of His mercies. Wherefore let us now pray to Him that thy footsteps fail not in thy passage through the Valley of Death.

All kneel, facing East

Ch. Ad.: Oh Lord of Strength, Elohim Gibor, in all humility of spirit we invoke Thy blessing. Look down, we implore Thee, upon this Postulant, who now kneeleth before Thee and knocketh at the gates of the grave. Grant him Thine aid, oh God of Israel, who givest power unto Thy people. Pour forth Thy benediction, we beseech Thee. Oh Thou Fire-hearted One, who dost send death that we may attain unto life everlasting; Thou at whose Word the thunders roll and the darting lightning flashes forth, grant that in the midst of storm we may find peace. Master of the Diadems of Fire, crown him with light, that, emerging from the darkness of the tomb, he may enter upon the dawn of endless day! AMEN.

A pause. All rise and chief adept points to the tat pillar from which **3rd Ad.** *takes bowl of water to place in Postulant's hands.*

Ch. Ad.: Thus far, oh Postulant, hast thou climbed the Mountain of Abiegnus, even the sacred mountain of initiation. Thy feet have trodden paths, steep indeed and narrow, yet clearly marked by those who have gone before thee. At every step, friendly hands have been stretched out, ready to aid thee;

friendly voices have spoken encouragement in thine ear. Now must thou step forward alone into the darkness of the grave, remembering that it hath been said, "I have trodden the winepress alone." To each one who seeketh the Light cometh the period of darkness–that Dark Night of the Soul of which the saints have warned us. To each cometh a time when the soul must receive the purification of absolute negation before she can hear the command "Enter thou into the joy of Thy Lord;" that purification of which the piscina of our earlier ceremonies is the foreshadowing. Noble Lord of Eventide, place the bowl of water in the hands of the Postulant, that he may behold his face as in a glass darkly.

3rd Ad. *does so, instructing postulant to bend his face and look steadily at the reflection.*

Ch. Ad.: Behold then, my frater, thyself submerged, even as of old the postulant was held beneath the waters of baptism until he entered the gates of death, emerging then, and then only, purified from the stains of Earth. Thus must thou also purify thyself, body and soul, in darkness and in silence before thou canst pass along the path of Purgatorial Fire, of which the Southern Pillar is the emblem, to that resurrection which we in patience hope for. No man liveth to himself and no man dieth to himself; rather each gathereth in the life of his fellows, even as a mirror gathereth images of all around it. The still mirror reflects truly and the living mirror perfects the unequal image. No troubled image finds therein its rest; for it restores that which was broken and that which it sends forth again is Peace. But to send forth Peace, first we must overcome, and herein lieth the watery of the double letters, as thou wast told that one letter and one Planet denote opposites. For in the Path of Mars indeed is found war and destruction, but in the Palace of Mars, which is Geburah, thou mayest find Peace.

3rd Ad. *replaces bowl and indicates Tarot key of Hanged Man.*
2nd Ad.: Herein, my Frater, you may perceive somewhat of the same symbolism, under another similitude. In our system of correspondences the Tarot key of the Hanged Man is attributed to the Path of Mem, and in the teaching concerning the Tarot which you have already received, you have learned that the signification of this key is sacrifice. But there are other and deeper significations than this, since the Hanged Man (under which title we may remember that our Lord was "hanged upon a Tree") is also entitled the Drowned Giant, and in this likeness may be said to refer to the Adam Kadmon of the Kabbalists–the ideal man who reflects the image of God, even as thy face was but now reflected in the bowl of water. And herein is a great mystery, for in each of us is submerged that image, but oftentimes so distorted by the waves of tempestuous passion that it is unrecognisable save to the discerning eye of the Adept, whose vocation it is to utter the word of Power, "Peace, be still." In the act of Creation, it may be said that the Supreme sacrificed Himself by imposing certain limits, whereby He was thenceforward bound in manifestation, even as the Word conformed to the limitations of humanity in His incarnation.

Therefore must we also offer ourselves as a living sacrifice, holy, acceptable unto God, which is our reasonable service. The 23rd Path of Mem is called the Stable Intelligence, and it is so called because it has the virtue of consistency among all numerations.

2nd Ad. *returns to his seat and* **Ch. Ad.** *comes forward and points to the key of Justice.*
Ch. Ad.: The path of Lamed, you have already learnt, is attributed to the Tarot key of Justice, which leads from the Beauty of Tiphareth to the Severity of Geburah, and it may

thus be said to denote the equilibrium between emotion and will. It represents, as you see, a queen seated upon her throne, her foot resting upon a fox, her hands grasping a sword and a pair of scales. Thus shall the Soul, upheld by the firm will, tread underfoot the desires of the flesh, and rule her kingdom by the Light of the Spirit. "Mercy and Truth have met together, Righteousness and Peace have kissed each other," and in that embrace shall spring the Perfected Man, ready to face with tranquil mien whatsoever the day may bring forth, life or death, joy or sorrow. The 22nd Path of the Sepher Yetzirah is known as the Faithful Intelligence, and it is so called because by it, spiritual virtues are increased and all dwellers on Earth are nearly under its shadow.

The **Ch. Ad.** *moves to east of altar.* **2nd Ad.** *hands him the censer.* *3rd adept slips cowl over postulant's eyes and lights the 33 candles. Remove Tarot keys.* **2nd Ad.** *&* **3rd Ad.** *take their places south and north of altar, each with an extinguisher. The temple is in darkness save for the candles.* **3rd Ad.** *removes cowl and cloak (from Postulant).*

N.B. The following four paragraphs given by the **Ch. Ad.** explaining the symbolism of the altar and the thirty three candles are not usually read out during the ceremony. *(These were considered optional—with a preferred use by Taylor. PZ)*

Ch. Ad.: Behold how the mystery of the 33 lights upon the white gold Altar. The Altar itself, as you may perceive, is of rhomboidal form, implying thereby that you have consecrated your whole being to the Divine Inspiration. The five lights in the midst are the five senses and their red colours donated the passions of which they have been in the past been the vehicle, while their exalted position signifies their purification through sacrifice.

The two pairs of brown candles are the somatic divisions, while the two sets of four are the four Zoa and the four Angels of Revelation which have their counterparts in the Yetiziratic and Briatic worlds, as green is the ethereal counterpart of earth.

The two-three symbolise the six divisions of the RUACH in the Qabbalistic divisions of the soul, the logos or Microprosopus.

The seven are the seven Chakras, the seven steps to Throne. And finally, the three single lights are the three divisions of the Higher Soul or Spirit: Neschamah, Chiah and Yeschidah.

Ch. Ad.: I am the Great One, Son of the Great One; I am the Fire, the Son of Fire: I have knit Myself together, I have made Myself whole and complete; I have renewed My youth: I am Osiris, the Lord of Eternity. Thirty-three are the centres of Life in My Body, thirty-three were the years of My Life upon Earth; at the end thereof did I relinquish My material life upon the Cross of Tiphareth. I am the Word spoken in silence. I am the Anointed of the Lord. Nine are the letters of My Name.

2nd Ad.: Homage unto Thee, oh Lord of the Starry Skies: and of the Aeons of the Bornless beyond. Thou art more glorious than the Sun in its rising, Thou who didst sacrifice the life of the flesh.

3rd Ad.: Oh grant unto me a path whereon I may pass in peace, for I am just and true. I have not spoken lies wittingly, nor have I done aught with deceit.

2nd Ad. & 3rd Ad. *put out four brown candles.*

Ch. Ad.: He that believeth on Me believeth not on Me but on Him that sent Me. And he that seeth Me seeth Him that sent Me.

2nd Ad.: Homage unto Thee, oh Soul of Everlastingness;

Thou Soul Who dwellest in Eternal Light. Thou art Lord of life and death, for Thou hast died unto the passions.

3rd Ad.: Oh grant unto me a path whereon I may pass in peace, for I am just and true. I have not spoken lies wittingly, nor have I done aught with deceit.

2nd Ad. & 3rd Ad. *put out four red candles.*

Ch. Ad.: I am come a Light unto the world, that whosoever believeth in Me should not abide in darkness.

2nd Ad.: Homage unto Thee in Thy dominion over the luminaries; the Diadem of Fire encircleth Thy brows; Thou art the One who maketh the strength which protecteth us, and Thou dwellest in peace above all, for Thou hast died unto the Body of the Stars.

3rd Ad.: Oh grant unto me a path whereon I may pass in peace, for I am just and true. I have not spoken lies wittingly, nor have I done aught with deceit.

2nd Ad. & 3rd Ad.: *put out four green candles.*

Ch. Ad.: I am the Vine, ye are the branches. He that abideth in Me and I in Him, the same bringeth forth much fruit; for without Me ye can do nothing.

2nd Ad.: Homage unto Thee, oh Lord of the Vineyard; Thou turnest back the worker in evil and causet the vine to bear fruit: for Thou hast shed the blood of Thy desires.

3rd Ad.: Oh grant unto me a path whereon I may pass in peace, for I am just and true. I have not spoken lies wittingly, nor have I done aught with deceit.

2nd Ad.: *puts out red light in centre.*

Ch. Ad.: I have glorified Thee on Earth, I have finished the work which Thou gavest me to do: the glory which Thou gavest me I have given them, that they may be one.

2nd Ad.: Homage unto Thee, who art beautiful at morn and at eve: the never resting stars sing hymns of praise unto

Thee; the stars which never fail glorify Thee, for Thou art dead unto sin.

3rd Ad.: Oh grant unto me a path whereon I may pass in peace, for I am just and true. I have not spoken lies wittingly, nor have I done aught with deceit.

2nd Ad. & 3rd Ad.: *put out 7 violet candles.*

Ch. Ad.: I have declared unto them Thy Name and will declare it, that the love wherewith Thou hast loved Me may be in them, and I in them.

2nd Ad.: Homage unto Thee who art crowned King of Kings, oh the Divine Substance. Thou sendest forth the Word and the Earth is flooded with silence at Thy Renunciation.

3rd Ad.: Oh grant unto me a path whereon I may pass in peace, for I am just and true. I have not spoken lies wittingly, nor have I done aught with deceit.

2nd Ad. & 3rd Ad.: *put out 6 yellow candles.*

Ch. Ad.: These things have I spoken unto you that in Me ye might have peace. In the world, ye shall have tribulation, but be of good cheer. I have overcome the world.

2nd Ad.: Homage, unto Thee, Thou Prince of Peace; the souls of the east pay homage unto Thee, and when they meet Thy Majesty they say "Come, come in Peace."

3rd Ad.: Oh grant unto me a path whereon I may pass in peace, for I am just and true. I have not spoken lies wittingly, nor have I done aught with deceit.

2nd Ad.: *puts out 4 green candles (above this was done by* **2nd Ad. & 3rd Ad.** *together).*

Three candles now remain alight. **Ch Ad.** *takes the white one and faces east, still swinging the censer; one blue one at each side remain.* **2nd Ad. & 3rd Ad.** *lift aside all the rest, leaving space for postulant to pass through.* **Ch Ad.** *leads the way into vault, places light on pedestal and* *gives censer to* **3rd Ad.** *and cloak.* **Ch Ad.** *passes to south. Postulant stands west of the pastos.* **2nd Ad.** *stands beside him, takes strip of linen and winds it slowly round him as* **Ch Ad.** *recites sentences, binding brow, lips, heart, solar plexus and hips. Six bells sound.*

Ch. Ad.: *(for brow)* Be not curious in unnecessary matters, for more things are shown thee than thou canst understand.

(for lips) Be silent, oh man, before the Lord, for He is raised up out of His holy habitation.

(for heart) Woe be to the fearful heart and faint hands, and to him that goeth two ways.

(for solar plexus) The greater thou art, the more humble thyself, and thou shalt find favour before the Lord.

(for hips) To know the Lord is perfect righteousness; yea, to know His power is the root of immortality.

The bandage being now on, **Ch. Ad.** and **2nd Ad.** assist postulant into the pastos and lay him down, head to north, hands crossed at wrists, palms up, above his head. They sprinkle salt over him.

2nd Ad.: So shalt thou rest in peace.

Ch. Ad.: Until the day break and the shadows flee away.

PRAYER OF COMMITMENT

Ch. Ad.: Oh Thou who makest perfected souls to enter into the everlasting glory, cause now, we beseech Thee, the perfected soul of this our Frater to be victorious over death. Having ears, may he hear with understanding; having eyes, may he perceive the spirit; having lips, may he speak the truth; having a heart, may he love righteousness. Quicken in him, oh Divine Creator, the Life Divine, draw him with cords that he may run after Thee, bind him to the Altar that he may evermore serve Thee. Amen.

They withdraw from the Vault, leaving the door slightly ajar. The Vault is in darkness, save for the candle. The hours are sounded and sentences for the 36 hours are read outside.

1. I will both lay me down in peace and sleep; for Thou, Lord, makest me to dwell in safety.
2. Thou wilt keep him in perfect peace, whose mind is stayed on Thee, for he trusteth in Thee.
3. He giveth his beloved sleep.
4. When thou liest down, thou shalt not be afraid, yea thou shalt lie down and thy sleep shall be sweet.
5. Though a man shut his eyes to the last, still cometh Death, the Render of the Veil.
6. If thou hadst known how to suffer, thou wouldst have had the power not to suffer.
7. The Place of Rest, the Home of Peace, is in truth the very Cross itself, the firm foundation, on which the whole creation rests.
8. I have torn myself asunder, I have brought unto them the mysteries of light to purify them, for they are the purgation of all matter.
9. Blessed is the man who crucifieth Malkuth and doth not allow Malkuth to crucify him.
10. Blessed is the man who knoweth the Word, for he hath brought down Heaven and bound the Earth and raised it heavenwards; and he becometh the midst.
11. Watchman, what of the night?
12. The morning cometh and also the Night. If ye will enquire, enquire ye.
13. I sleep, but my heart waketh.
14. The heart sleepeth; who shall wake it? The wind of dawn hath stirred the night, day is near.
15. The morning is my messenger; rise thou up and greet

Me; the night is also from Me, bless Me and rest.

16. Of the Universal Aeons there are two growths, without beginning or end, springing from one root, which is the Power of Silence, invisible, inapprehensible.

17. The Mystery which is beyond the World, whereby all things exist, because of it all Mysteries exist and all their regions.

18. Cease not to seek, day and night, until thou hast found the purifying mysteries.

19. Before the eyes can see, they must be incapable of tears.

20. Before the ears can hear, they must have lost their sensitiveness.

21. Before the voice can speak in the presence of the Masters, it must have lost its power to wound.

22. Before the feet can stand in the presence of the Masters, they must be bathed in the heart's blood.

23. One is the nature below, which is subject to death; and one is the race without a King which is born above.

24. And he cried "A Lion". Behold I stand continually upon the watchtower in the daytime, and I am in my ward whole nights.

25. And He said," I am thou and thou art I, and wheresoever thou art, I am there I am, in ALL am I sown.

26. Wheresoever thou willest thou gatherest Me, and gathering Me, thou gatherest thyself.

27. I shall be merciful to thee in the Cross of Light.

28. Rejoicing, I come to Thee, Thou Cross, the Life-Giver, Cross whom I know now to be mine; I know Thy Mystery, for Thou hast been planted in the world to make fast things unstable.

29. Until the day break and the shadows flee away, I will get me to the Mountain of Myrrh and the Hill of Frankincense.

30. The people that walked in darkness have seen a great Light; they that dwell in the Land of the Shadow of Death, upon them hath the light shined.
31. For on this Mountain shall the hand of the Lord rest.
32. He will swallow up death in victory, and the Lord will wipe away tears from all faces.
33. Who is this that leadeth them but she that dwelt in darkness and in silence? Whose coming is as the beauty of the beloved when the Sun shineth out from clouds.
34. Pilgrim of the day, go forth and meet in every face the Risen One. If He wake, He will greet thee, and thy portion shall be double; if He slumber, hail Him in silence; wake Him not. He knoweth His own hour and God is over all!
35. Thy dead men shall live; together with my dead body shall they arise. Awake and sing, ye that dwell in dust; for thy dew is as the dew of herbs.
36. Hold no longer silence, cry ye aloud for the beauty of the Divine Mother; for in Her is Peace.

There is a pause. **Shekinah** *appears from behind the curtain in the northeast with the alabaster lamp and spray of acacia. She bends over Postulant and kisses him on the brow, saying;*

Shek.: Arise, shine, for thy light is come, and the glory of the Lord is risen upon thee.
3rd Ad.: *turns up lights. Shekinah lays acacia on postulant's breast, then anoints him on his feet, solar plexus, lips, brow, and palms of hands, saying:*
Feet: The Life of the Tree is thine–arise and walk,
Solar plexus: The Life of the Man is thine–receive and give.
Lips: The Life of the Word is thine–utter and love.
Brow: The Life of the World is thine–receive the spirit.
Palms: The Life of the Stars is thine–be filled with joy.

There is a pause, then Shekinah removes acacia, moves to the foot of the pastos and says:
Shek.: The place of hiding is opened, thy place of hiding is revealed. Behold, thy soul hath dwelt in darkness; let her now return unto light. Thy spirit withdrew unto the stars, which never diminish, return to bring power to thy soul. Thy brow is like unto the King's, thy lips are opened, thy heart is upon its throne. Thou hast knowledge, yea movement is restored unto thy hands and feet. Thy Father dwelleth in thee, oh son of the most high. Thou art the Son of the Great One and thou hast seen the hidden things. Thou shalt not die a second time, for thou hast gained the mastery. Arise, then, and come forth, that in the Power of Silence thou mayest save mankind. I send thee forth, fail not, nor falter, but remember that which thou hast received.
Turn up light in vault. **Shekinah** *withdraws.* **Ch Ad. & 2nd Ad.** *enter vault.* **Ch Ad.** *goes to the east,* **2nd Ad.** *stands at west. They bend down and take Postulant's hands, placing their free hands behind his shoulders and thus assist him out of the pastos.* **2nd Ad.** *removes the bandages, while the* **Ch Ad.** *says:*
Ch. Ad.: Hail, hail unto thee who hast died; rise up ...... thou hast embraced thy bones, thou hast gathered together thy flesh and blood; Elohim Gibor guardeth thee; Elohim Gibor strengthened they hands; yea He guideth thy feet; thy lips are opened, thou hast received thy head; thou hast received thy soul, and thy spirit hath returned to thee from the stars which never diminish.
They lead postulant out of the vault so that he stands just outside door, **Ch. Ad.** *at south,* **2nd Ad.** *at north.* **Shekinah** *comes to door behind him. Water drops from her raised hands onto his head.*

2nd Ad.: Happy is he who hath looked upon the place of rest; the waters shall not overwhelm him. (Doulos Siges) Parapedemes de Vallis, Server of Silence, shall be his name.

Ch. Ad.: I am the Lord of those who are raised up, who came forth, out darkness.

Postulant: (*as prompted by the* **2nd Ad.**) I have entered in as one who hath no understanding. I have come forth as Lord of Life through the beautiful Law.

Ch. Ad.: & **2nd Ad.** *turn and face Postulant.* **2nd Ad.** *shows two signs.*

2nd Ad.: Behold, thou shalt turn away nine eyes from evil, even as Nephthys turned away her face from the Destroyer of Osiris; and thus shalt thou withdraw thy soul from temptation, even as Isis, withdrew from darkness.

Ch. Ad.: (*shows the grip*) Herein is reflected the five powers which have been restored to thee. It is the Sign of the Mighty One–Blessed be He–even of Elohim Gibor, the Lord of Strength. Twenty is the number of his name.

They turn to the Postulant, facing east and all kneel at the door of the Vault. **Shekinah** *stands within the door holding the butter, honey and milk. As she offers butter and honey, they all make the sign of Nephthys; as she offers milk the officers make the sign of Isis.*

Shek.: Butter and honey shall ye eat, that ye may know to refuse the evil and choose the good. Desire ye the sincere Milk of the Word, that ye may grow thereby.

They remain kneeling in silence. **Shekinah** *withdraws to the east. Long pause. Turn out the vault light. Light fades.*

Ch. Ad. *rises and closes the door of the Vault.*

Ch. Ad.: In the name of Elohim Gibor, depart in peace, for

the **Shekinah** hath withdrawn Herself. *He faces east and exclaims:* **Shekinah**, Thou Queen of the East, forget not thy sons. Tabanu, Taboona, dwell in our souls. Queen of the Dawnland, Bath Qol, speak to our spirits, that we might go with thy blessing. Oh thou, Beautiful Daughter of Light!
After a long pause, **Ch. Ad.** *stoops and raises the Postulant in silence and the* **2nd Ad.** *leads him out.*

6=5
CUES FOR POSTULANT
Part One

Postulant is robed in white; black cord around waist, black cowl overhead, black slippers. Carries Hierophant's Lamen. After preparation by **3rd Ad.** the Door is left ajar. On hearing a bell sound twice, Postulant *knocks once hesitantly.*

On hearing the words "East of the Sun and West of the Moon," *he knocks more firmly.*

On hearing the words "his pledge is duly maintained," *he knocks thrice urgently.*

3rd Ad.: opens the Door and asks by what right he enters. The Postulant silently offers Hiero's Lamen.

On entering, a question is asked; the answer is *the Sign of Osiris Slain.*

Later on, another question is asked, ending: "signify thy name with the Sign of Light." Postulant makes *Lux Signs in Silence.*

At each clause of Obligation, Postulant bows head in silence in assent.

Part Two

Postulant has feet bare, save for red slippers, and purple cloak. He carries the Admission Badge of Scales.

Personal 6=5 Notes

Just after receiving the 6=5 from Taylor, he insisted that I start an analysis of the 6=5 Ritual while the ritual was still fresh in my mind. Taylor gave me a few points to start the analysis in the form of headings, to which I appended a series of following notes. The idea behind this was to use this as a baseline for future analysis over the coming years and as I grew with experience then the understanding would be a lot deeper. I have left this initial set of notes intact to show where I first started as it has been about 35 years since I first went through this ceremony and looking back on them I see how naïve I was at the time. Needless to say my understanding of this ritual has changed greatly compared to what I originally wrote. Everyone has to start somewhere in ritual analysis, and this was it for me. After about 15 years I decided that this ritual was not the model I wanted to use and I drafted my own 6=5. The problem I had with the Felkin 6=5 was threefold. The first was that it did not go further in the Vault–as an extension of the 5=6. The second was that the Rosicrucian element was paid lip service to and there was no real exploration of the third important manifesto: *The Chemical Wedding of Christian Rosenkreutz* with its solid alchemical theme. If we followed the original Mathers structure of learning then I envisaged the 6=5 to be a study of the Portal and the 5=6 a study on the 7=4. The Babe of the Abyss would be the study of the 6=5 Ritual and the 8=3 would be a study of the 7=4 Ritual so all these rituals had to be soundly constructed with that concept in mind.

Quite recently I found out that Mathers had used the 6=5 to study the 5=6 Ritual thus combining the Portal and 5=6 in one unit, which it was originally. The view that I took was that to properly analyse the Portal ritual one would have to be grounded in alchemy and its effect in ritual, which would take a whole level of learning in itself. The Felkin 6=5 is still a powerful ritual and is being used in some temples today. Whatever its shortcomings are, it is still structurally better organised than the Mathers Alpha et Omega 6=5.

NOTES ON THE SYMBOLISM OF THE 6=5 RITUAL
By Pat Zalewski

Preparation

Before the start of the ritual, the Shekinah pricks her finger and mixes her blood with that of olive oil saying: "Blood is the life of man; let the man give his life." This symbology is very complicated, and at more than one level. Olive oil is under the Goddess Athena (which also means vulva or womb) who presided over voyages. In order that a person can be made new or life given to him, he must pass into the land of the unborn. It is the voyage of the spirit seeking his eternal roots. With the introduction of blood, we have the Melusine, an entity who has the capacity to cure diseases and change shape, and is a form of regression wherein she becomes what she was in the beginning of man: a part of his wholeness. This shows the aspect of transformation the aspirant must undertake to complete the journey in safety.

The Wands

These wands are the same as those in the 5=6 Ritual, but because they are well above the Veil, their symbolism is altered to suit the level of the 6=5 Grade.

Chief Adept's Wand

This is the Yechidah, "The divine spark that is in me more than myself; the deepest layer of consciousness." This is one of the highest forms of manifestation of the Kabbalistic Soul. It equates to Kether, and hence is a blueprint for the entire Tree in a balanced format, as shown by the Winged Sphere (soul) balanced between the forces of good and evil (the two serpents).

Second Adept's Wand

His wand is the Chiah or "Essential Will, the creative impulse of Yechidah which through it attains its realization." On the Tree, this Chokmah (Wisdom) or masculine force of the Great Father.

Third Adept's Wand

This wand is the Neshamah, and corresponds to Binah; the Great Mother: symbol of understanding.

The Officers

These have been associated to what some collectively call the Neshamah, or the upper spiritual plane of the three phases of the soul, which has two further groupings within it (Yechidah and Chiah). All of these are motivated by the Zelem, the divine spark behind each phase of the soul. The Officers in this Grade are the Zelem of the upper three phases, or the guiding force, while the wands are like the soul, the first manifestations of that impetus. Collectively they are the highest levels of the soul, synthesized together in a working format in archetypal terms.

Opening

The opening vibration that activates the link to the Second Order is its divine name "Rose Rubea Et Aurea Crucis" which is then transmitted to the individual by touching the Rose Cross. This also equates to establishing the link to the Second Order through the Vault by way of the lightning flash. With the word "Elohim Gibor," is the second vibration, which summons the Archangel Khamael and the Angelic Choir of the Seraphim to assist with the ceremony.

The secret number 20, refers to the gematria of the second vibration "Elohim Gibor" and also stands for the 20 Princes of the Enochian Tablet of Union, a complete synthesis of spirit on the Enochian level. These are linked to the 63 Kerubic Emblems (the 16 subdivisions of each Elemental Tablet) 64=Dyn–Justice–a title of Geburah. Both 20 and 64 equate to 84=Enoch, the first human recipient of the Enochian Tablets. Also, the 20th Key of the Tarot is Resh, the Sun: the symbol of balanced polarity outside the boundary of human limitation; the beginning of the divine realm.

The third important vibration is in the Chief Adept's proclamation: "In the strength of Elohim Gibor" which opens the link specifically to the Mars Wall of the Vault.

When the Adepts place the ends of their wands in the Pastos, they formulate through the higher aspects of the soul, a Ka or Astral Shell, which has all the vibrations of the 6=5 Level. This is turn taps its vibration from the Mars Wall and is contained by the Pastos. This Shell remains in the Pastos, and is tuned to link with the vibration of whoever lies within, which links his aura with that of the vibrational pitch of the 6=5 Grade.

The wands are joined above the Pastos. The Chief Adept's wand is Yechidah=28=unity or union. The 2nd

Adept's wand as Chia=23=separated. The 3rd Adept's want is Neshamah=390=Firmament or Heaven. This equates to "Unity of the separated heavens." When all the divisions are added up they are 28+23+390=441=Truth.

Emblems

The Emblem is the three Ankhs touching above the Pastos which is associated to the Three Mother Letters: Aleph, Shin, and Mem. The formula of the first manifestation, 1+400+300=701=The World. This is all of creation in a composite form. Applied to the archetypal world of the Tarot, a complete story is formed from the Three Tarot Cards with the Mother Letters on them. Aleph as the Fool is the Divine Child, and birth under difficult conditions. Mem then carries on the theme of life itself; enlightenment through suffering. Shin is resurrection, as the rewards for the quest of life. In the final part of the opening, Shekinah appears veiled with a lamp under the veil. This shows that the unknown quality of the sphere, the feminine anima, is present, to be summoned forth from the deeper layers of the psyche.

First Point

The Postulant is robed in the white of spirit which symbolizes the overall vibration he experienced in the Vault at the 5=6 Level. *The first knock* is a symbol that the unification of the Neshamah with the Ruach and the Nepschech was obtained in the 5=6 Grade. *The two bells* are the Yechidah and the Chiah, the two stages of the soul he has yet to experience.

The reception of the Postulant with the words: "Heat and burden of the day," allude to the solar power of Tiphareth, and the knowledge and work that went with that Grade. The place of rest "East of the Sun and West of the Moon" is shown on the Seal of the Order of the R.R. et A.C. and refers to the sacrifice man must make to advance in the Order.

The second knock shows that the Postulant has attained the knowledge of the Second Order and has the right of admittance.

The third knock of three batteries shows that the Postulant is ready to experience the unification of the three higher phases of the soul.

Three bells sound—the unification has begun. Also, it shows that the restriction imposed on the aura (by impregnating the aura with the elements during the Outer Order Rituals) is now removed, and the aura and astral body can now expand to encompass the higher vibrational energies.

The Venus Wall is pointed to by the 3rd Adept. The answer alludes to the entrance being solar, the point of Tiphareth on the Tree where the 5=6 is reached before entrance to the Vault is given. Daleth, as Venus, is the 14th Path on the Tree, and equates through gematria to "Earth of Geburah," which signifies that one must experience the Sphere of Geburah in the physical before one can advance to the spiritual level. The physical level so referenced is of course the 6=5 Ritual.

The Postulant is now prepared for the obligation, and has to affirm by way of agreement. The LVX Signs given by the Postulant are of course sign of his agreement to this.

The four bells are sounded. These related to the numerical value of the Door to the Vault (Daleth), which is the Path through the Vault and to the Sphere of Geburah.

Obligation

The obligation here is fivefold, representing the five points of the Pentagram. One is for each letter of the Holy Name (Yod, Heh, Shin, Vau, Heh) = 10 + 5 + 300 + 6 + 5 = 326, which equates to "Vision or Revelation" showing that the unrevealed will now be revealed. This reduces further to 11; the 11th Trump being Lamed, the Pathway to Geburah and the 6=5 Grade.

The Postulant is then censed in the form of a Pentagram, an archetypal geometric pattern symbolizing the oath he has just taken.

Second Point

The Chief Adept gives the challenge: "Who comes from Edom with dyed garments from Bozrah?" This shows that the Postulant has come from Edom=611, "The unlawful kingdom" or simply the uninitiated (to the 6=5 Level).

The reply he gives is a petition of how hard he has worked for this entrance. The Chief Adept now, in turn, petitions the angelic force of the Sphere of Geburah to accept the Postulant. They then emit a lightning flash to his aura.

The Chief Adept then hand the Postulant a cup of water, the symbol of passivity and reflection of the Self, which is the only way one can enter the 6=5 Grade. The water in the cup is Mem=40: "To bind." This shows the binding of the spirit that the Postulant has just received. This fact is also stressed by the Tarot Trump the Hanged Man (Mem), which also shows the binding force, but given in archetypal form. The Hanged Man (the 11th Key is numbered 12) which means "to penetrate," and indicates an understanding of the deeper mysteries. The Tarot Trump Justice is then shown which represents the balance of one's life energies.

33 Candles

The symbolism of the 33 candles has already been explained in the Ritual, but also the number of 33 equates to "Oil Vessel," in which the Holy Oil is poured. As each candle is extinguished, the oil symbolically fills the vessel (the Postulant), which is also shown in the preparation.

With the extinguishing of the *four brown candles*, one then finds that the Four Elemental Divisions of the body are left behind: "Thou didst sacrifice the Life of the Flesh."

The *four red candles* are then put out. These show that the fiery emotion has now been left behind: "Thou hast died unto the passions."

The *four green candles* are extinguished. Here, strength and weakness are left behind: "Thou art the one who maketh strength which protect us."

The *red light in the center* is extinguished. Here, the seed of desire is left behind: "For thou hast shed the blood of thy desires."

The *seven violet candles* are put out. All sin is transgressed here, so that a Path be cleared to the heavens so one may obtain the unobtainable: "O grant me a Path where I may pass in peace."

The *six yellow candles* are put out. Here a sign or some type of contact is asked for: "Send word and the earth is flooded with silence at thy renunciation."

The *four green candles* are put out. Here the petition is answered by the Chief Adept: "In the world (physical) ye shall have tribulation."

The whole process of extinguishing the candles is a symbol of the shattering of the physical sphere, so that the soul can be readied to ascend into the astral. The single candle is left lit, because it is the one link the Postulant has to the Earthly Sphere; if this is extinguished, the soul is torn asunder from the body, and will find great difficulty in returning.

The *two blue candles* stand for the devotion or watery aspect of the Venus Door by which one enters. The Postulant is bound in linen, symbolizing the auric envelope of the Astral Shell (already in the Pastos), which will impregnate his own aura.

Six bells are then sounded; one for the Kabbalistic Sephirah he has been initiated into. This also shows the number of Spheres in the Yetziratic World (including Daath), which is the framework one is currently working in.

Commitment

The Divine Force is then petitioned to receive the astral body of the Postulant through the link of the Second Order.

36 Bells

Each bell represents a decan in the Zodiac, and most important of all, a godform. The astral and soul in fact leave the body of the Postulant, and with each sounding bell, traverse the Zodiac which is representative of the soul's progress through the different forms of energy governing it, until a complete cycle is done. The Egyptian Zodiac has 37 decans: the first is the actual leaving of the body to meet this godform, while the next 36 are aspects of its journey. The 36 bells were rung to bring things in line with modern astrological studies.

With the appearance of the Shekinah, the Postulant meets the anima of the Sphere of Geburah; the hidden knowledge of that Sphere. The fivefold anointing of the astral body makes the centers aware in the astral (the five basic centers).

The Postulant is lifted out of the Pastos, and the linen around him is removed; he is reborn. The Signs of Nephthys are given: the Signs of adoration on the left and right side. The claw grip shown symbolizes the Postulant gripping the hands of the helpers, as he is lifted from the coffin.

THE MYSTICAL GRADE OF THE 7=4

Being the Grade of the ROD which BLOSSOMED

Officers:

THE MAGUS (**Ma.**): grey robe, white head-dress with a gold cord, leopard skin, sandals, spray of almond.

KING OF SALEM (**Kg.**): Blue and purple robe, winged sphere, lamen, incense, rose.

SHEKINAH (**Sh.**): Rose coloured tunic, black veil, Acacia

POSTULANT: (**Pos.**) 1. White tunic and red shoes. 2. Brown cloak and cowl, sandals and staff. 3. Robe of Glory. He must bring the spray of acacia received in the 6=5 and the crystal.

ANTE-ROOM: Draped in red, Pastos upright and draped in white. Portal Sand-coloured with cross of Lights, Ankh and Tat Pillars at the S&N arms of the Cross; tripod of salt in the West.

VAULT: Square, blue with a violet floor, grey veil across

EAST SIDE: White and Gold altar, black and white cross to fold up. Cauldron of bubbling water on the altar. Red Mars symbol on green curtain on the outer side of the vault door. Silver star is south of cauldron in the north. A lantern is placed by the **Shekinah** for postulant; the only tarot key that is painted is the Wheel of Fortune; the Hermit represents the postulant and Fortitude is shown by the **Shekinah** beside the lion.

FOUR STARS: Fomalhault, 12 rays, Antares, 24 Rays, Regulus 36 rays, Aldebaran, 72 rays.

THREE KEYS: Wheel of Fortune (revolving clockwise), Hermit (Brown Robe), Fortitude (Lion).

FOUR CORDS are required: amber, violet, black and silver.

OPENING

Vault door is wide open and curtains are drawn back; **Magus** *stand within holding a branch of pink almond blossom in his hand.* **Shekinah** *stands by the Tat Pillar with a spray of acacia in her left hand and a lighted lantern in her right.* **King of Salem** *stands by Ankh Pillar with a red rose in his left hand and a censor in his right. This forms a triangle with the* **Sekinah** *in the north and the* **King of Salem** *in the south.*

Ma.: The heavens open and the winds are still and let God's deathless sphere receive the WORD.

Kg.: Oh ADONAI HA ARTEZ, MELEK ISRAEL, Thou who appeared unto Moses in the flame of fire in the bush and gave him the law in Sinai–come and redeem us with stretched out arms.

He makes the Sign of Thoth

Sh.: OH SAPENTIA, PISTIS SOPHIA, Thou who came out of the mouth of the most high, reaching from one and to another, mightily and sweetly ordering all things, come and show us the way of Understanding.

She makes the sign of Hathor.

Ma.: Let us give praise to he who is sublime above the heavens and of every nature Lord

He makes the sign of Horus

All: OH CLAVIS DAVID , SHARBITH ISRAEL, Though who open and no made can shut, who shuts and no man can open. Come and bring the prisoner out of the prison house and him that sits in darkness out of the shadow of death.

All repeat the sign of Osiris and face East.

Ma.: El strong and Powerful. El, Lord of Light. Bestow on us thy grade that we in Unity with Thee may impart these Mysteries, which a Father only may bestow on a Son

Initiate so that he shall become an Eagle and soar to Heaven and Contemplate your Face. It is beyond his reach that being beneath the sway of Death he should unaided soar into the Height, together with the golden sparkling of the Brilliancy that knows no Death. Grant, we beseech thee, most Merciful, that he may be holy even as Thou art Holy, that being made one with Thee he may draw all men unto thee. Amen.

They prostrate themselves and touch forehead to ground thrice.

POINT ONE

Lights are extinguished and the door is set ajar.
Bell is struck four times.
Pos.: *approaches the door and knocks four times.*
Kg.: (Opens door wide) By what Key would you unlock this door?
Pos.: *holds out the spray of acacias and replies:*
Pos.: My brow is like unto the King's; my lips are opened and my heart is upon its throne.
Kg.: *clasps his hand with the 6=5 grip, holds his other arm firmly just above the elbow, draws him into the dark room and guides him backwards in a spiral to the anteroom; he places him upright in the pastos and then binds him around the knees with the amber cord.*
Kg.: The feet of Sothis are represented and you are born to their state of rest.
Around the loins with the violet cord.
Kg.: You have inherited Eternity and everlastingness has been bestowed on you.
Around the heart with the Black cord.
Kg.: There is nothing hid which shall not be made manifest, nor buried which shall not be raised.
Around the head with the silver cord.

You shall be aware that you are the Son of the Father and you know that you are in the City of God and you are that City. *Starting to revolve the wheel clockwise he withdraws, leaving the* **Pos.** *alone. The door is partly closed showing the Wheel of Fortune Key. One of the Officers reads clearly so that the* **Pos.** *may hear through the partially closed door:* Harken now to the Mystery of the Tarot Key before thee and meditate thereon in thy heart. Is not the tarot itself named from the Rota the Wheel of Destiny–of Birth and Rebirth. Do not the radii spring from the white centre of the Divine Spirit, passing into the darkness of the womb of the Divine Mother? Even as the Life of man, even as the Life of the Worlds also, which alike pass ever from the Divine Faith into the Divine Mother, that being born of the Virgin they may be crucified upon the Cross of Manifestation and thence commit themselves again upon the Cross of the Father. Man indeed stands between the Spirit and Matter, between the Angel and the Animal. At the summit of his ascent we behold as in a glass darkly, that the Perfected Being whom our Fathers strove to represent in the Sphinx, compound of the four elements in balanced disposition–the intelligence of Man, the soaring spirit of the Eagle, the Fiery Heart of the Lion and the firm stability of the Bull. Born of the Spirit he must descend to Malkuth until he is clothed in the coat of skin–the Body which is prepared for him by the humble brothers of the Flesh. And thence shall he arise again bearing with him that creation which groans and travels together with him until now, awaiting redemption. The Twenty-first Path is the Intelligence of Conciliation and it is so called because it receives the Divine Influence which flows into it from its benediction upon all and each existence.

There is a long pause during which the **Pos.** *must repeat to himself the Mantra given to him to learn in his preparation. While he does this he should continue to gaze at the revolving Wheel. In this interval the lights of the cross are arranged in the Portal and the tripod of salt is placed just within the entrance form the anti-room. The four stars much also be put ready. The green one by the salt, the blue on the tat, the Red on the Ankh and the silver within the Vault.*

Mantra

Earth born and bound, our bodies close us in, Clogged with Red clay, and shuttered by our sin –We must arise. Flowers bind round and grasses catch our feet, Bird songs allure and blossom scent is sweet–We must arise. Mountains may beckon and the seas recall: Cloud-forms delude and rushing streams enthral–We must arise. Planets encircle with their spiral light, Stars call us upward to our faltering flight–Thus we arise. Sun-rays will lead us higher yet and higher, Moon-beam our souls scorch with their purging fire, Thus we arise Into the Darkness plunge, fearless of pain; Coldness and silence cleanse us again– Still we arise Open ye Gates of Light, Doors open wide; Gaze we within at the Glories you hide–We have Arisen.

Kg.: *enters and opens the door but does not withdraw the curtain. He points to the brown cloak, sandals and staff which lie on the floor and says:*
The Ascent of the Mountain of Initiation must eve be toilsome. Each of us must pass through the Dark Gate of Death

before we can attain the summit. Each must treat the fiery path of purgatory, tracing again therein the rescuing symbol of the cross marked therein by lines of flame by the lion of Fortitude. And to do this the initiate must also be the Hermit, the dweller in the desert, the pilgrim clothed in the brown habit of the earth, yet supported by the firm staff of steadfast will and aspiration seeing the light of inspiration which in due season he will receive from the hand of the Great Mother a spark of the Indwelling Glory which ever halls the holy places of humanity. Thus may he loose the binding cords of desire and lust, that he may truly dedicate himself body, soul, life and spirit to the living service and thus may he exchange the robe of Earthly Darkness for the wedding robe of Glory and attain the beatific vision. The 20th Path of the Sepher Yetsiarah is called the intelligence of Will and it is so called because it is the means of preparation of all and each created being and by this Intelligence of the secret of all the activities of Spiritual Beings and is so called because of the Influence diffused by it from the most high and exalted supreme Glory.

POINT THREE

The Postulant should, without prompting step forth from the Pastos and take the brown cloak and put it, and the sandals on and take the staff in his right hand.
One bell sounds.
The door opens revealing a lion in the open doorway. Behind him stands the **Shekinhah** *a lighted lantern in her hand. She holds this out to the* **Pos**.
Sh.: He that would be the greatest let him be the Server
Pos.: *makes the 6=5 signs and lays his hands on the head of the lion. He takes the lantern and says:*
Pos.: Server of Silence is my name.

Shekinah *withdraws and the lion disappears thus revealing the tripod of salt.* **Pos.** *kneels on both knees, sprinkles salt on himself and says aloud*:

Pos.: Earth to Earth and body to body–in the name of ADONAI HA ARETZ Lord and King of Earth, I dedicate my body to the Service of the Highest.

He loosens the amber cord from his knees and lays it across the Salt. King of Salem comes forward and fastens the Green Star on his left knee and says:

Kg.: And behold a Star in the West even Fomalhaut in his brightness and his rays shall be a guide to your feet.

Tripod is removed. **Pos.** *moves forward, entering the Cross of Light. He passes betten the lines of light until his way his barred. He turns to the Tat Pillar with the bowl of water on the Top and a cup of white wine on the blue arm. He takes the cup and wets his lips with the wine and then pours the rest into the bowl of water. He falls onto the left knee and cries:*

Pos.: Water to Water and Soul to Soul in the Name of the Great Mother I dedicate my Soul to the Service of the Highest.

He loosens the Violet cord from his lions and hangs it across the Tat. **Sh.** *Comes forward and binds the blue star around his waist and raises him saying:*

Sh.: Peace, Peace until him that is near, Let the Light of So-this bring peace to the Soul.

Pos.: *turns and goes to the Ankh pillar. He sprinkles incense on the flame and falls on his right knee and cries:*

Pos.: Fire to Fire and Life to Life in the Name of Jah, everlasting , I dedicate my life to the service of the highest.

He loosens the Black Cord and throws it through the loop of the Ankh. King of Salem comes forward, raises him and binds the red star across his breast saying:

Kg.: Thy Heart is as the Heart of the Lion, and the Star of the King, even Regulus, shall burn on your Breast.

Pos.: *turns back and is directed to approach the entrance to the Vault where the scarlet Mars on Green curtain hands. He raises the lantern on high, last his staff across the threshold before the curtain and cries:*

Pos.: Light to Light and Spirit to Spirit in the name of that which not be uttered, I dedicate my Spirit to the service of the most high.

The curtain is withdrawn and **Shekinah** *stands within the Vault. Her veil is now thrown back and she holds in both hands the crystal sphere upon which is the sigil of the* **Pos.** *is engraved or painted.*

Sh.: I am He and He is I and Lo! The Creator has placed your crystal sphere within the starry heavens.

She gives him the sphere, takes the lanten and places on the right side of the altar. She then turns again and lossesn the cord about his brow saying:

Sh.: Let the Silver cord be loosed.

She lays the cord across the left side of the altar and takes the silver star and puts it about his brow saying :

Sh.: I have give unto thee the starry crown of Aldebaran that you may pass on to the Heavenly Path.

POINT FOUR

King *enters Vault and directs* **Pos.** *to kneel in the doorway of the vault and draw the cowl of the pilgrims robe over his eyes. There is a pause.*

At the end of this time the bell sounds.

Pos.: *is raised to this feet and dawn across the threshold with the 7=4 grip. The brown cloak is taken from him and laid aside. At his feet lies, a cross of Six squares and beyond this is the altar.*

Kg.: The Father has given a commandment and the Son has made for me a spiritual body through his own soul. I am he who has travelled far and who has made the pilgrimage among the stars of heaven and to the Heart of the Great Mother. She gave birth to me because it was Her will to do so. I am Osiris, the first born of the Gods I have become a Divine being. I have renewed by youth as the Eagle. Behold I was watched and guarded but now I am released. Behold I was bound with cords but now my Crystal sphere is within the starry heavens. I have knowledge and I have Truth and movement is restored to my hands and feet. I have passed through the Gate of Fomalhut, I have come forth from the Star Stothis. I have received the heart of the Lion. I am crowned with the Crown of 72 rays. Now let my soul be called into Thy presence and my spirit be lain upon the altar. Oh my Father I have come before Thee and Thou have caused me to enter the hidden Abode. Strengthen Thou me as Thou has strengthen Thyself and show Thyself to Thy Son. Oh Thou who returns and withdraws Thyself, let Thy will be done.

Sh.: Oh Mystery which is without the worlds, because of which all has come into existence, this is the whole outgoing and the whole upgoing which has emanated all emanations and all that is therein, because of which all mysteries exist and all their regions. Come unto me, oh Thou who returns and withdraws himself. Come unto us for we are your limbs. Come unto us for we are all One with Thee. We are all one and the same. You are the Father and we draw nigh unto Thee, that you may receive this your Son. Strengthen him as you have strengthened Yourself and show Yourself to him that Your will be done. We clothe this, your son, in the shining robe of glory!

She puts the Robe on him and points to the cross on the floor.
Sh.: The last shall be first and the lowest shall be the highest. Malkuth shall be exalted into the Throne of Kether and all shall be consumed and become infinite and holy. The stone which the builders rejected, the same shall become the corner stone. The Cross of suffering is transmuted to the corner stone of the arch and raised above the Earth. The son shall offer that which he has received.
Sh.: And peradventure then shall he behold the face of his father.
The **Pos.** *must fold up the Cross into a cube and kneel on it supported by the* **Sh.** *And the* **Kg.** **Pos.** *Holds his crystal in both hands and bends his head. There is a pause and then the* **Magus** *appears behind the veil.*
Ma.: Be still my son. Here the praise giving that keeps the soul in tune–the Hymn of Rebirth–The song of Union, Be still my Son.
Thus shalt you know that He is Himself Both things that are and things that are not. The things that are He made manifest. He keeps things that are not in himself. He is the God beyond all name. He the unmanifest. He the most manifest. He whom the mind alone can contemplate. He visible to the eyes as well. He is the one of no body. The one of many bodies. No, rather He of Everybody. Nothing is there which He is not. For all are He and He is all. Be still my son.
Kg.: All are Thee. All are from Thee. O Thou who gives all and takes nothing. For You have all and nothing is there which You have not. You are what ever I may be. You are what ever I may do. You are what ever I may speak. For You are all and there is nothing else which you are not.
Sh.: You are that which does exist and you are that which does not exist. You are Mind when You think and Father

when You make and GOD when you energise and Good and Maker of All.

Ma.: Be still my Son. For I will sing the praise of Him who founded all. Who fixed the Earth and hung up heaven. Who rules the sea. Who makes the fire to shine. It is He who is the Eye of the Mind. May He accept the praise of all our powers. Oh Life and Light, from us to Thee our praises flow Father. I give thanks to You the energy of all our energies. Take back from me the all into Thyself. From You, from Your will–to Thee the all. The all that is in us–oh life Preserve! Oh Light illumine! Oh Creator Inquire! Father of Lights in who is no shadow of turning receive Thy son.

Pos.: *drops the Crystal into the Cauldron and raises his head. The veil is slightly parted and the* **Ma.** *touches the* **Pos.** *on the heart, lips, eyes and brow with the almond branch and then lays his hand for a moment on the head of the* **Pos.** *There is a pause. Then the Officers help him to rise and then the* **Kg.** *shows him the signs of the Grade.*

Ma.: Son remember you have given your all even to the uttermost. There can be no separateness for thee. Bear this in mind when I give you the watchword of the Grade which is ACHAN which signifies Unity and the two numbers 13, which is the number of ACHAD and 31 which is the number of El, the Divine name of this Grade. And both these numbers conceal the number 4 which is manifestation. And I greet thee as MENES THEOROS the abider (Dweller) on the mountains. Remember then Oh Son that in thee shall be manifest the Unity of the Divine One. And in token thereof, let us call upon him in the fourfold, mystic and terrible.

Kg. *tells the* **Pos.** *to remain kneeling at the altar as long as he desires The Veil closes and the Magus withdraws and all leave the Vault.*

GENERAL NOTES ON THE 7=4 GRADE

1. THOTH I will contemplate. (*Sign of the Word brought down to the soul from the central realisation thereof.*)

2. HATHOR With my right hand I will reach up to heaven, and my left hand I place upon earth. (*A sign of him who having ascended into heaven is desireous to draw things after him.*)

3. HORUS I will turn away from Evil. (*Casting out Image of matter: active detachment.*)

4. OSIRIS In Silence. (*He who sees in the great silence, the dawning Truth.*)

THE FOUR CORDS:
    Amber: declares the Mystery of souls yet unborn.
    Purple: the Mystery of Incarnation.
    Black: Mystery of Death.
    Silver: Mystery of Eternal Life.

PATH TETH: Gives power of utterance. It is the Vibrating Path.

OSIRIS: Right forefinger on lip: I will keep silence within. Completes 0=0 sign: I will keep silence, without.

PATH YOD: The word in the course of formulation, or expression.

KAPH: The uttered word.

SIGN OF VIRGO: Signifies Divine Inspiration in activity. Union of Tiphareth and Chesed.

CENTRAL THOUGHT: Unifying Human with Divine. Each form is dissolved into something better. Humanity becomes Divine Man. Order is a Path to this Union.

Note: Mantric formula of the Hexagram Ritual; Affirmation of Unity: Use it daily, recite at close of meditation.

ACHAD RASH ACHADUTHA RASH YEYEHUDA TEMURITHA ACHAD

One in His Personality,
One in His Individuality,
In His Permutation One.

The Nails of the 7=4 Cube

16 Nails thou shalt take to transform the CROSS into the CUBE. To steel shall thy be transformed from the natural Iron; by Fire and hammer, cold welded, and wrought till they are fit for service. So the natural desires of man be transmuted into Divine Virtues that thy whole being may become a living stone in the Temple of our God.

Passion is thus transmuted to Patience, that Patience may accomplish perfect work.
Lust becomes Love, ready to give all to the Beloved.
Drunkeness becomes ardent hunger and thirst: gluttony after righteousness which shall receive fulfillment.
Fearfulness is lost in Faith.
Wavering and instability become steadfastness.
Self-righteousness is swallowed up in Righteousness of God.
Pride becomes humility.
The rain glorious become as a chill.
The hard of heart become merciful.
Violence becomes meekness.
Malice becomes charity.

Wrath becomes peace making.
Dishonesty is forgotten in Supreme Truth.
Darkness is overwhelmed by Light, till the Ego of Humanity merges in the Selfhood of God.

PASSWORD: Abider in the Mountains
MENES THEOROS. SIGNS 4

HORUS: Casting out the image of matter.
OSIRIS: Silence
THOTH: Contemplation
ATHOR: Reaching up to Heaven and down to earth.

THE WHARE RA TEACHING OF 7=4

The Postulant's sphere is gradually developing from the first admission into the Order. At Grade of Chesed, it is clearly differentiated in all its parts, but there must be further purification before one can advance and pass the Veil dividing the Supernal Triad from the lower seven Sephiroth.

The symbolic sphere dropped into water has double significance: it is boiling and scented.

In modern surgery, boiling is a purifying process. All germ of evil is destroyed and in this symbolic act, the Postulant offers all that he has attained for ultimate purification; but he must not only be purified but etherealized and raised to a higher plane. The spirit of transmutation of the physical into the resurrection body. Herein the significance of the perfume and the spiritual connotation of the sense of smell: a sense which more than any other, reaches those mysterious centres which link the physical brain with pictures stored up in the sphere of sensation which we name "memory," and which is one of the peculiar attributes of SATURN.

The time between the Grades of Chesed and Daath should be a time of retrospection; of reviewing the past and seeking to trace the long hand of the Father Divine guiding and directing throughout the labyrinth of Fire.

Recall the concluding exhortation of the Magus: the injunction to remember and bear in mind, and recall also, the password of the Grade "ACHAD" which is "UNITY"; and realize, not only the Unity of God, but also the Unity of Man.

PREPARATION FOR 7°=4°

(The preparation extends over a four week period.)

1. **Burn** incense daily.
2. **Eat** beans, peas ("Pulse" of the Bible), purple grapes, honey, milk, white bread.
3. **Learn** thoroughly and **repeat daily** the following:

Earthborn and bound, our bodies close us in.
Clogged with red clay and shuttered by Sin: We must arise.

Flowers bind us round and grasses catch our feet
Bird songs allure and blossom scent is sweet: we must arise.

Mountains may beckon and the seas recall enthrall
Cloud forms delude and rushing streams: we must arise.

Planets encircle with their spiral light
Stars call us upward to our faltering flight: Thus we arise.

Into the darkness plunge, fearless of pain,
Coldness to silence cleanse us again. Still we arise.

Open Ye gates of Light — Door, open wide
Gaze we within at the Glories Ye hide; we have arisen.

4. Get a spherical **rock crystal** (Moonstone will do), and have Sigil of 6=5 Name painted on it.

5. Write **thesis** (1000 words) on resurrection and life after death.

6. Meditate 40 minutes daily (may include prayer).

7. Visit Vault regularly.

8. Study **Tarot Keys**—FORTITUDE, HERMIT, WHEEL OF FORTUNE, STRENGTH.

PREPARATION DURING THE 4 DAYS IMMEDIATELY PRECEDING ADVANCEMENT

Spend this in some form of real isolation, or retreat, if possible, on a height.

Bathe ceremoniously with hot water and a little soda or NH_3.

Learn the following correctly for the ceremony. *(No prompting.)*
a) Server of Silence is my name.

b) Earth to Earth and Body to Body. In the Name of ADONAI, Lord and King of the Earth, I dedicate my Body to the Service of the Highest.

c) Water to Water and Soul to Soul. In the name of the GREAT MOTHER, I dedicate my Soul to the service of the Highest.

d) Fire to Fire and Life to life. In the Name of JAH everlasting, I dedicate my spirit to the service of the Most High.

e) Light to Light and Spirit to Spirit, In the Name that may not be spoken, I dedicate my spirit to the service of the Most High.

Note: An Officer in the ceremony indicates at which stage these sentences are spoken.

Cues for Postulant

1. When the bell sounds 4 times, he will approach the Entrance.

2. When asked for his passport, he must reply: "My brow is like unto the Kings; my lips are open; My heart is upon its throne."

3. He will be led into the room with the 6°= 5° Grip, and must walk backwards when required.

4. When he is left alone and in silence, he must repeat to himself the whole of the Mantra he has already learned; during this time he must keep his eyes upon the Wheel.

5. Let him remember that the Path of Fortitude can be trod only by the Hermit.

6. Let him understand that when a door is opened, he should prepare to pass through it; he who seeks will find that which he requires.

7. When he receives the Light, he must say "Server of Silence is my name."

8. Only he who hath dedicated his body may obtain communion with his soul: "Ye are the Salt of the Earth." He who renounces Joy, pouring out the wine into the water, shall savour the sweetness of Life. He who shall offer himself as incense cast into the flame shall approach the Sanctuary, but before entering therein, he must dedicate even his innermost spirit.

THE ETHERIC LINK

Flying Roll 39

One of the most little known but important facets of the Order is the "Etheric Link," for without it there can be no Order. The Link itself is in three stages. The first is its development in the Outer Order.

In the 0°= 0°, the Neophyte is first introduced to the Link, which results in a type of power surge in the aura which expands the aura and heightens its density. It is seen by those who are clairvoyant as a shimmering green or blue light (depending on the degree of contact). In the four subsequent Elemental Grades that follow, the Link established in the 0°= 0° is then opened up to receive an impetus of energy tailored to, and in empathy with, the corporeal elements. At this point the aura must be continually charged through ritual practise and meditation, exercise, so that the power-flow through the Link does not close or seal off, which it will do if left in the outer Element Grades for too long a period. (For example, spending a couple of years on each Element Grade.)

If an individual is expelled or leaves the Order in the Outer Grades, the Link will automatically seal itself off, as it cannot be sustained without impetus from the Second Order, no matter how much study is done.

From the Portal onwards the Link undergoes a definite change. Being parasitic by nature, it forms a firm shell within the aura itself, which resembles the shape of the body. It is translucent and emanates through the aura from subtle centres of the body. Once accepted into the body during the 5°= 6°, it is impregnated into the individual for life, unless the Chiefs who emanate the Link choose to close it down. In the Order one can only reduce the Adept in rank to the

Portal, but they have no power to alter or cut the Link. If one advances through the Second Order Grades, this Link is further strengthened by ritual.

In the final phase at the 7°= 4° Grade, a Ritual called "Transmission of the Etheric Link" is performed (and is usually reserved for those of the Office of Chief or who will succeed to that Office), where the Link is given in its entirety to the Adept so that they are able to carry on.

The Link, in its varying stages, could be described as an astral tunnel of sorts, allowing access to certain regions of the astral plane where a contingency of astral entities govern their respective areas. The main theory is that if there are enough links to humankind, more energy is released to man to accomplish things of the "Great Work." Hence, when one obtains initiation with an Order, these links are forged. Basically, this is a two way communication. The astral entities need devotion to increase their own power in the astral (by having the devotee send back the impetus through devotion and worship), with the result being the energies of two different worlds are received and converted: a type of perpetual motion that increases as long as both parties are willing to conform.

Each Esoteric Order usually works from an essential basic theme, but concentrates in different areas of development. When a link is formed, one attunes to working in a particular area to which the astral entities have been designated (from their own plane) to develop.

Direct contact with these astral entities is done via the Link (astral tunnel), in which the Adept travels during skrying trips to those planes he wishes contact.

There are a number of instances where Adepts, once in the Second Order, find that through their astral abilities they are attracted to entities to work in areas other than the Order. In cases like this, the Guardians have consented to accept them so that they can progress to a certain level; then another Link is forged from that point to another set of entities or esoteric Order. It must be remembered that even in the astral, there is a certain amount of give and take. In algebraic terminology, "A" must go through "B" to arrive at "C." The Christian faith is a good example of this as are the numerous off-shoots of our own Order. In a case like this, once the new Link at "C" is formed, the old one at "B" is closed, and a direct link from "A" to "C" is utilized.

The Transmission of the Etheric Link
Chief Adept   2nd Adept   3rd Adept

Ch. Ad.: "V.H. Third Adept, who is he that waiteth without the Portal?"
3rd Ad.: "Our Frater et Soror......, who hath attained unto the High Grade of ......"
Ch. Ad.: "Go then, V.H. Associate Adept, and see that it is in truth our Frater ......Test him if he be well prepared to proceed with this ceremony, being in a calm and recollected frame of mind, that we may bestow upon him in full power the Link which we have commissioned to transmit to him."

Instruct him to enter this hall of the Adepti, his hands meekly folded upon his breast; let him say clearly and humbly, 'I...... hereby request you to bestow upon me the true Etheric Link which unites us in unbroken succession with our Founder and Father Christian Rosenkreutz and His Companions. May he transmit therewith the Spiritual Knowledge and Power of Healing and Comfort to the sick and sorry, and may I be enabled to use those gifts for the good of the Rosicrucian Order to which I have the honour to belong. I pledge myself to use this Link according to the Ancient Traditions of the Order, and I proclaim my sincere belief in the person known to us as Christian Rosenkruetz, who founded the Order to which I have the honour to belong.'

"**V.H. 2nd Ad.**, assist the **3rd Ad.** in the Reception of our Frater."

3rd Ad.: Goes out, prepares the Postulant, and sees that he is robed in White, and he gives him the petition, and guards the Portal.

Postulant gives !!! !!!

2nd Ad.: Admits them.

Pos.: Reads petition.

Ch. Ad.: "V.H. Frater et Soror, since the days when our Founder and Father C.R.C. dwelt upon this Earth, He has been able, by His great advance, to exercise supreme rule over the Order called by His name. He and certain of His followers who have passed through the Veil, form a circle which continuously directs the growth and development of this Order, aiding its Rulers and inspiring them. At intervals of 120 years, this supervision becomes for a time more definite, and has been used to modify and reconstitute that it may be constantly adapted to the needs of each new age.

In the year of Our Lord 1890, this revival and reconstitution of the Order took place. Under the new conditions, no written mandate was issued to the Rulers of the Temples or Groups, and it is therefore more necessary that the purely Etheric Link should, at the discretion of those who already hold it, be transmitted to such Rulers and Adepti as may be considered suitable. For this reason it is now offered to you. We have been given the Power to transmit it and the privilege of conveying it to you, and through you to others who may be judged worthy. We do this therefore on the understanding that you will exercise due care and conscientious discrimination in the transmission of this Link to others;

that in doing this, you will call to your aid Two Fraters who have also received it from us, so that you form a Triangle of Power. Should one of the three be removed from this plane, let the remaining two select a discreet and loyal person as successor. You are only empowered to transmit this Link to member of the R.R. et A.C.

"In receiving this Link and those Higher Grades which we are in a position to bestow upon you, you will in truth become connected with the modern successors of the Original and True Rosicrucian Order. That Order which was founded in Europe in 1250, and was duly manifest in 1405 as is transcribed in our Ritual of the 5°=6° Grade.

"I now charge you to answer truly under those conditions.

"Are you willing to receive this LINK, and never to reveal when, where, or from whom you have received it?"

Pos.: "I willingly accept the conditions and pledge my honour that I will faithfully observe them."

Ch. Ad.: "Approach then the Vault, my Frater, and kneel within its Threshold while we invoke our Father Christian Rosenkreutz."

Chiefs *enter the Vault and* **Pos.** *follows and kneels on the Threshold facing East.* **Ch. Ad.** *stands East of him, facing East.* **2nd Ad.** *in South East.* **3rd Ad.** *in North East. They stretch out their right hands towards the Centre East holding their Wands.*

Ch. Ad.: "CHRISTIAN ROSENKREUTZ"
2nd Ad.: "CHRISTIAN ROSENKREUTZ"
3rd Ad.: "CHRISTIAN ROSENKREUTZ"
ALL: "CHRISTIAN ROSENKREUTZ, we invoke Thee to manifest Thyself and to transmit through us the ETHERIC LINK with thyself to this our Frater...... that he may indeed become Thy son and spiritual heir."

There is a pause.
The three Officers turn slowly, form a Triangle about the **Pos.**. *They lay aside their Wands and Ankhs.*
Pos. *is directed to place his left hand on* **Ch. Ad.**'s *breast, his right hand in the* **Ch. Ad.**'s *right hand.* **2nd Ad.** & **3rd Ad.** *place their hands: one on the head of the* **Pos.** *over* **Ch. Ad.**'s *left hand, and the other on* **Ch. Ad.**'s *back.*
All: "I (we) by the Power transmitted to me (us) do hereby transmit to you Frater...... the ETHERIC LINK with our Father CHRISTIAN ROSENKREUTZ, and the Rosicrucian Order founded by Him.
There is a pause.
Adepti withdraw their hands and leave the Vault. **Pos.** *remains kneeling. The Door is closed upon him, and he is left alone for 10 minutes. The* **Ch. Ad.** *then goes into the Vault, raises* **Pos.** *by placing his hand on his head, saying:*
Ch. Ad.: "May you be brave. May you be faithful. May you be true."
Note: The Pastos should be placed in the Portal for this Ceremony and the Altar moved to the extreme East; and Three Candles placed upon it. The incense should be burning.
All present exchange the Full Grip across the Pastos, then form a circle and do full 7=4 Signs.

APPENDIX I

THE EQUINOX CEREMONY

The Equinox Ceremony is one that very little information has been published on, and as a result many of those in charge of some Golden Dawn Temples do not realize its full worth. In fact, I know of one G.D. Temple head who wanted to perform the Ceremony a week after the event, which showed a lack of understanding of its essence.

While people have their auras continually charged by the Order's Ritual, the Order itself, as a Group Soul, also needs charging; by this I do simply mean the astral contacts with the Chiefs. The Equinox Ceremony literally draws down the Power, so that contact by the Guardians of the Order can be made with strength. Also, for those present, the astral links are made stronger, and their benefits are multifaceted. On the lower side of things, the auras are recharged, with a magnetic force that will help in matters of health. Our own links to the Guardians are then made closer, which then opens up new levels of consciousness for us. We draw directly on the Solar Power as well, directing it to a desired end. The various currents of the godforms become hyper-active, and their energy force is more easily manipulated.

Generally, the Chiefs of the Order will retire to the Vault after the Equinox Ceremony, and make their contacts and take directions from those entities they come into contact with. The following notes on the Equinox are published for the first time, and has all the hallmarks of being written by Felkin. At any rate, regardless of who wrote it, the main thing is the explanation of the esoteric aspect of Ceremony.

What occurs during these contacts with the Equinox, has been described by clairvoyants as traveling through a set of tunnels, whose walls are like nets, acting to hold back the negative forces that are trying to prevent one making contacts.

Notes on the Ceremony of the Equinox

This Ceremony is proceeded by the Opening of the Temple in the 0=0 Grade, the full significance of which is realized only very gradually as we advance in the Order. A hint about the purpose of the Opening is given in the Hierophant's speech.

Let the number of Officers in this Grade and the nature of their Offices be proclaimed once again; that the powers whose images they are may be reawakened in the spheres of the those present, and in the Sphere of this Order.

For by names and images are all powers awakened and reawakened.

Great and normally hidden powers are evoked and manipulated by those who consciously act as their representatives for the benefit of the Candidate or, as in the Equinox Ceremony, for that of all the members present. It is therefore against this background of heightened consciousness that the Cosmic Drama of the Equinox is enacted.

The Equinoxes are the two points where the ecliptic, i.e., that apparent path of the Sun through the heavens, intersects the Celestial Equator at an angle of W 23 degrees 27 minutes. (The Celestial Equator is the projection on the Heavens of the Earth's Equator.) Since from an occult point of view, this Celestial Equator is a projection into Cosmic Space of the Spiritual Life Centre of the Earth, the importance of the Equinoctial points becomes at once apparent. It is here that the Spiritual Life of the Earth becomes vitalized and renewed through its close contact with the Spiritual Fire of the Sun. We do not know the meaning of this Mystery (Cosmic), except in so far as it is reflected in Man.

Twice a year, at the Vernal (March 21st) and at the Autumnal Equinox (September 23rd) there is a unique opportunity for a spiritual renewal. Though the Ceremonies are the same, the quality of the Spiritual Life which is poured out differs at the two Equinoxes. In Spring, the Sun enters the Sign Aries which is ruled by Mars, who tinges the Sun's Fire with his restless out-going energy which searches outwardly for the means of self-expression and self-enrichment.

In Autumn, the Sun's entry into Libra stirs into activity the opposite influence of Venus. It is no longer the life of the personal self which is of importance, but the unifying influence of the Planet of Love which impels us to search for that other–our Higher Self–and to prepare for that inner consummation which will lead to rebirth and a new life.

We may remember that after Winter Solstice, we celebrate the birth of Jesus during this half of the Solar Year.

The coming six months are therefore under the influence of the Spiritual Life of Union. It is thus in a sense dual or, rather, under the influence of a duality which should be merged into unity or oneness.

Our Ceremony is a presentation of this Solar Drama showing its effect on Man, and its interpretation lies chiefly with Kerux, (silent though he is), and Hegemon.

It might be helpful to remind ourselves of the meaning of these two Officers in the 0=0 Grade.

Before the Equinox can be ushered in, the existing Password is abrogated, denoting the end of a dispensation.

Old links are broken, and the stage is set for the reception of a new life, bringing with it a new relationship.

This is done by Kerux, the executor of the Will of the Hierophant. There now takes place an interchange of Force between two pairs of Opposites: Light and Darkness–Heat and Cold.

Irreconcilable on the physical plane, each pair of opposing forces is yet merged into one harmonious channel through the balancing action of the Hegemon.

As representative of the Spirit, she stands at the Centre of the Universe. The opposing Forces from East and West and from South and North go through her. She gathers them up into herself, and by adding the essence of the Spirit, transmutes them and sends them out again in one united ray.

In this way, first the transverse line is established from East to West, then the longitudinal bar of the Cross is added from South to North.

If we refer this Cross of the Tree of Life, then the line from East to West binds Kether and Malkuth together, while the transverse bar unites the two Pillars. The four extremities are thus gathered into one Central Point in Tiphareth, symbolized by the Hegemon, the centre for receiving and transmitting opposing forces; thus she becomes the Reconciler.

As soon as the Cross has been established, a Circle is precipitated around it by the naming of the Four Aspects of the One: One Creator, One Preserver, One Destroyer, One Redeemer. This figure is the symbol for Earth.

Hegemon again emphasizes the reconciling Central Point of the Spirit: a fourfold manifestation, yet one in origin.

Now we come to the second point of the Ceremony when each Officer, beginning with the Hierophant, lays down his insignia of Office on the Altar, and takes from it his appropriate symbol. A great deal lies hidden in this action.

At the Equinox, as one particular influence is fading out, so each Officer voluntarily relinquishes his emblem of Office, the symbol of power of his soul. The last action he performs under the influence of the current password is a willing sacrifice offered up at the centre of his own being.

The four Officers who symbolize the two great opposites, always find the symbol of their respective element in balanced disposition on the Altar, as each one of us finds them eventually in our own heart. The four in one are in perfect union. This whole action of turning inwards is symbolic of a change of consciousness; they cease to function as Officers on the Earth Plane, and become representatives of a Higher Power on the Cosmic Plane. One point must be noted here: all the Officers come to the Altar from the West, this side of the darkness of Malkuth and Matter. They are going up towards the East, and therefore reach a higher state of consciousness when they arrive at the Centre.

Hegemon is the only Officer who remains East of the Altar on the side of the Light, the motionless Spirit at the Centre of the Universe. There she awaits Kerux.

Kerux is the only Officer who carries two insignia, a Lamp and a Wand. A significant action takes place when he reaches the Altar. He gives up his Wand, The Rod of Power; but the Light with which he has shown others the Way of return to the Spiritual Centre, he returns to its source.

He hands it from Darkness to Light across the Altar into the safe keeping of the Hegemon.

In the 0=0 Grade Kerux represents Man, the Alchemist, who in the beginning is the homeless wanderer intent on his search for the Philosopher's Stone.

Gradually, he brings the Candidate to the goal of his secret quest, aided by the ray of light from his own spirit, dim and faint though it is. But now he must sacrifice even his own spiritual light. It is only when he has renounced his own individual spirit that the Higher Powers can be moved into action.

For Kerux this represents a kind of death...the death of the Self. He realizes that he himself is nothing and can do nothing, and that all his abilities and powers, together with his separate spiritual self, must be sacrificed.

Then, in silence and without prompting, he sets out from the North on a higher spiritual quest; after the sacrifice, follows a conscious new orientation of the Will towards the Higher in a spirit of silent submission. It might help us to understand the next point in the Ceremony if we recall that the Celestial Equator is, occultly speaking, a projection into Cosmic Space of the Spiritual Life Centre of the Earth.

This has just been symbolically enacted by the four Officers who take their Elemental Symbols from the centre to the circumference, here representing the Celestial Equator.

We also recall the speech of Hiereus in a higher grade, beginning with the words: "From the Centre outwards so moveth the point as it traceth the Line and the Cross."

This bears out the fact that our Order Mysteries are not only of human, but also of Cosmic Significance.

Kerux now takes upon himself the character and function of the Spirit of the Earth, who twice a year, by virtue of its position, comes into the closest contact with the Sun from whom it receives new life, tinged with the quality of either Vernal or Autumnal Equinoctural Sign.

Though Kerux no longer carries his insignia, he still wears his Lamen depicting the Caduceus, Symbol of Healing, infused with the Spirit of his Higher Self at the proceeding Equinox. He is therefore marked out for redemption, whether we look at him as the Spirit of the Earth or as that of Man living on the Earth.

Emphasis must be laid on the fact that the willingness to receive the new spiritual influx must first be demonstrated by Man before the Higher Powers can perform the work of transmutation in him. This is the reason why the four Officers wait silently till Kerux faces them. He, as it were, impels the Spiritual Powers of his Soul to turn outwards towards the vast Cosmic Force, which at the Equinox sends new life and strength into the world of men.

This new Life is broken up into four streams of Power before it reaches Man. With a prayer and adoration, each Officer receives the appropriate new quality of that Force, and fixes it with the Sign of the Cross in the Sphere of the Temple. As each Power affirms his particular aspect of the One Spirit, Kerux, as the carrier of the Light, precipitates it into a Circle. Already the four opposing Powers have been brought to a point of union at the Centre of the Universe in Tiphareth. The way now lies open for the unimpeded down pouring of the Spirit from Kether to Malkuth, thus establishing the Middle Pillar of Beneficence. (It would take too long to discuss the Cosmic implications of this Great Mystery.)

First the Hierophant draws in the Light to Kether with the words: "Holy art Thou, Lord of the Air, Who hast created the firmament," the firmament being symbolically situated above Kether. Dadouchos, as the Guardian of Fire, invokes the Lord of the Fire: "Wherein Thou hast shown forth the Throne of Thy Glory": A clear reference is made here to the Sun on its Throne in Tiphareth. Hiereus praises the Lord of Water: "Wherein Thy Spirit moved at the beginning," being the Waters of Creation of Yosod. The Stolistes in the place of the greatest symbolic darkness, fittingly addresses the Lord of the Earth: "Which Thou hast made Thy Footstool."

In this way, bringing the Light right down to Malkuth, thus completing the Middle Pillar.

It is of importance here that throughout this part of the Ceremony, Hegemon should hold the Lamp. For as she in common with all present turns to the four quarters, the new Life passes through Kerux to her, and she in turn transmits it to the Lamp, symbol of the Spirit of Man; a Ray of Divine Light. Let us remember that this renewal and completion of the Spiritual Life could only be effective through a preliminary act of renunciation.

The Circumambulation of Kerux lays down a Circle of Light on the Cross of Foundation established in the first point of the Ceremony. The two symbols together represent here the Sun, crucified in space, sacrificing His life so that Man may live.

Hegemon, having received the new Life, acknowledges the Oneness of the Spirit underlying its fourfold manifestation, and with the newly charged Lamp of Life, consecrates the symbols of the powers of the soul offered up on the Altar.

When the newly appointed Officer later on take up their insignia, they do so with the inner feeling and realization that the powers of their soul have been strengthened and enriched.

On completion of this point, the Chief confers of the new password by the power and authority vested in him.

Just as the Sun at the Equinox, by the authority of the Universal Spirit, imparts a new rate of vibration or quality to the Life Force which is poured through, so does the new password give it direction. Herein lies its importance.

After the new Hierophant has been installed, he conveys his aspect of the new Spiritual Force through his hand to the Lamen of the Officers and consciously asserts its new direction by claiming their insignia with the password.

One brief word about making of the Neophyte Sign to the Altar and the four quarters. Here it is symbolic of receiving the new Spirit and passing it on again, in this way laying emphasis on the fact that Man is a channel for the Higher Forces, which must be freely given out just as at the Equinox the Cosmic Spirit pours Itself out for the healing of mankind.

APPENDIX II

THE PORTAL OF THE ROSY CROSS

The following Ritual of the Portal is by Waite, and is one of those he sent to Felkin in 1910. It has been included as a matter of interest to the reader. The Portal, though on the edge of the Inner Order, is considered the first of the Inner Order Rituals, and this to date unpublished one is of particular interest. If one compares the Tarot descriptions of the Waite cards in the Ritual to those given in his Tarot book, one will find new dimensions in the cards. Overall he did not structurally alter the Rituals from the old Golden Dawn, but changed the phrasing to suit his own style. It was, in my opinion, change for its own sake.

Felkin admitted in *The Wayfaring Man*, that he was jealous of Waite. By the 1890s, Waite's research was considerable by anyone's standards, and even though one tries to read his books without going to sleep in between the phrases, they do contain a great deal of knowledge from the Alchemy of Paracelsus, the Zohar, and the Grimoires; his writings were certainly broader in scope than those of anyone else in the G.D., the two possible exceptions being Mathers and Westcott. Felkin found that many of the G.D.'s Inner Order members used to ask Waite's help and advice, and was generally looked up to. On the other hand, Felkin and Company were more practical magicians than theorists, which is what I conclude Waite to have been. By noticing the changes he made to the original rituals and deducing the motive behind them, I am sure that he did not understand the practical magician's outlook; if he did, it is not betrayed in any of his writings after the period he joined the Inner Order.

In the late 1930s, Mrs. Felkin tried to get some of the papers Waite held in joint trust with her late husband, but her letters to him were ignored, and hence many of the documents that should have gone to Whare Ra were never sent despite the legal entitlement of this Temple to them. The same applied to Miss Felkin, who tried to get the documents from Mrs. Stoddard, who was, in the modern vernacular, "completely out of her tree" by this stage.

Quite recently, I was in touch with a fellow Australian author who claimed 7=4 descent from a member of Waite's old Temple, though he informed me that he never activated the Order in Australia when he returned there from England. Since Waite was always rewriting his rituals, it is difficult to pin him down to a particular ritual style: some of his speeches being no more pompous than several in the original G.D. parlance. The Christian element though is very strong throughout most of his ritual invocations, albeit thinly veiled.

If Waite could be accused of anything, it would have to be the broad scope that he had to work with. Hence, one could speculate as to the problems he must have encountered in the Golden Dawn. If he would have joined in with the others instead of trying to take over the lead, the Order could possibly be flourishing today in renown fashion. Nevertheless, Waite's contribution to the G.D. should not be ignored. For it was Adepti like him that gave the others hope to carry on with the Work when all could have crashed about them, even though that hope was limited to a short span of time.

THE PORTAL OF THE ROSY CROSS

Issued by the Authority of the Concealed Superiors of
the Second Order to Members of the Recognized Temples
Privately Printed 1910

THE HIGH OFFICE OF OPENING THE HOLY PORTAL

The Temple is arranged for the Opening and for the First Point, as follows:

The Portals of the 23rd, 26th, 24th, and 21st Paths are placed in the East. The 13th, 14th and 15th Tarot Keys are shown at conventional stations therein. The Diagram of the Paths and Grades is laid upon the Altar, which is in or near the middle part of the Temple. The Pillars are to the West of the Altar at a mean distance between the Altar itself and the Table. The latter is placed as far West as the exigencies of the Ceremony will permit. Thereon are the Four Elemental Tablets, with the Tablet of Union in their centre.

The Throne of the East is occupied by the Celebrant of the Grade, who is saluted in the Ceremony by the title of Master of the Portal. He wears the crossed sashes of the Outer and Inner Orders, the white robe of the Second Order, the yellow cloak of a Cancellarius, an ordinary Nemys and a Rose-cross on his breast, the Rose being of five red petals. He has no Second Order insignia. For the clearing of the Temple he uses the Sceptre of a Hierophant.

The Officers of the Outer Order, wearing all vestments and insignia, are seated thus:—

The Kerux is in the far West, with the Stolistes and Dadouchos on his left and right respectively; their seats are close against the wall. They represent the position of Malkuth on the Tree, and they correspond to the Grade of Zealotor, in which the earth part or body of man is purified. The Hierophant is on a seat a little distance in front; he corresponds to the Grade of Hegemon and Hiereus are on seats South and North of the Altar, facing East; the answer to the Grades of Philosophus in Netzach and Practicus in Hod respectively, or to the will and the emotions. On low pedestals beside them are the emblems allocated to each of the Chief Officers—the Fan to the Hierophant, the Cup of Water to the Hiereus, the Lamp to the Hegemon and the Vessel of Salt to Kerux. The Stolistes has the lustral water and aspergillus of his Office and the Dadouchos the Thurible, from which incense rises.

If the Temple has not been opened previously in any Grade of the Outer Order, the ceremonial clothing of Officers takes place in the manner prescribed by the Ritual of the Neophyte Grade, and the clearing follows as usual. It is done by the Celebrant-in-Chief, as representing the higher consecration of the Second Order.

It should be noted that as technically and sometimes actually the Officers of the Outer Order are not all of the 5=6 Grade, so therefore in this Ceremony, which cannot be witnessed by any below the Portal of the Rosy Cross, they are not all of necessity those appointed at the last Equinox and holding positions therefrom.

The Prayer at the East having been recited, if necessary, the Celebrant turns to the West, but remains in place. The Stolistes comes up, following the course of the sun, and hands him his Vessel for consecration, according to the prescribed form of the Neophyte Grade–unless so consecrated already. Thereafter the Celebrant turns to the East, having the Stolistes on the left side of him. He takes the aspergillus and sprinkles water in the East.

Celebrant–Pure waters and holy waters; wells of the Waters of Life: in the Name of the Living Waters.

He passes to the South, carrying the aspergillus and followed by the Stolistes with his Vessel. He sprinkles thrice in the South.

Celebrant–Influx descending from *Binah*; Waters of Understanding: in the Name of the Great Waters.

He performs the same Ceremony at the West.

Celebrant–Cool water and still water; fountain which never ceases: in the Name of the Waters of Contemplation.

He performs the same Ceremony at the North.

Celebrant–Waters of Creation; Waters flowing back to their source; in the Name of the Waters of Sanctification.

He reaches the East for the second time, lifts up the Vessel of Water, which he takes from the Stolistes, turns westward and says:

Celebrant–Behold I have purified water.

He gives back Vessel and aspergillus. He remains in his place. The Stolistes returns with the sun to his seat, while the Dadouchos rises and, following the course of the sun, brings up his Vessel of Incense, which he elevates before the Celebrant, who consecrates it according to the prescribed form of the Neophyte Grade—unless so consecrated already. The Celebrant turns to the East, having the Dadouchos in his left, from whom he takes the Thurible and offers incense in the East.

Celebrant–Fire which comes down from above; Fire in the World Supernal: in the Name of the Fire which enkindles.

The Dadouchos takes the Thurible and follows the Celebrant to the South, where the same ceremony is performed.

Celebrant–Fire which rises upward; Fire of the soul's aspiration: in the Name of our Fire of longing.

He performs the same ceremony at the West.

Celebrant–Fire of the outward splendour; Fire of the Indwelling Glory: in the Name of that Fire which is *Shekinah*.

He performs the same ceremony at the North.

Celebrant–Fire of purgation in *Geburah;* Holy Fire of Judgment: in the Name of Perfect Fire.

He again reaches the East, lifts up the Vessel of Incense, turns westward and says:

Celebrant–Behold I have consecrated with fire.

He resumes his place on the Throne of the East. This is a momentary pause.

Celebrant–Fraters et Sorores, of the Holy Order of the ∴∴, Brethren of the Concealed Sanctuary, I say unto you that the Light is extended, that the channels of its communication are free and fair and gracious.– ק – Assist me, I pray you, to open the Secret Door which leads from the Grade of *Theoricus*, by a Path of Temperance and Prudence, to the Hidden Portal in *Tiphereth*, and the Sanctuary of the Second Order. *All rise.*

Celebrant–Honourable, *Frater Kerux*, Lampbearer of the Outer Order, Guardian of the Gate of the Wise, assure yourself that those present have received the offices of mercy which are conferred upon all who have opened the Gate of *Samech*, have traversed the Middle Path.

The Kerux comes up with the sun to the East of the Altar and faces West.

Kerux–Truly Honoured *Fratres et Sorores*, give me the Sign of the Portal.

It is so done accordingly.

Kerux–This is the answering Sign. *(He gives it.)*

The Kerux, who carries his Wand only, turns to the Throne of the East.

Kerux–Master of the Portal, they have made their dwelling in Jerusalem; they have passed from the Holy of Holies, through the divided veil, into the Hidden Temple of the Heavenly School.

He returns to his place with the sun.

Celebrant–Honourable *Frater Hegemon*, what is your symbolical situation in the precincts of the Portal?

Hegemon–In the South of the Temple, signifying the *Sephira Netzach*, the element of fire and the consecration of the will of man. I am in correspondence with the letter *Yod*.

Celebrant–Honourable *Frater Hiereus*, why are you placed in the North?

Hiereus–My seat is in the glory of *Hod*, which is a reflection from the light of our desire in Tephereth. I signify the element of water and the consecration of the emotions of man. I am in correspondence with the letter *He*.

Celebrant–Truly Honoured Hierophant, Expounder of the Lesser Mysteries in the Order of the .∴.∴., your station heretofore has been ever on the Throne of the East: why are you located at the western end of the Temple?

Hierophant–I await in the sphere of Foundation, in that holy sphere *Yesod*, the opening of the Gate of Samech—that he whom I have brought so far in our Mysteries may traverse the vertical Path, even to the Portal of *Tiphereth*. I signify the element of air and the consecration of the mind of man. I am in correspondence with the letter *Vau*.

Celebrant–Honourable *Frater Kerux*, what is your station in the Temple?

Kerux–Truly Honoured Master of the Portal, my place is in the nethermost West; I stand in the sphere of *Malkuth*; I signify the element of earth and the consecration of the body of man. The *Stolistes* and *Dadouchos* are beside me, bearing their mystical elements as symbols of the work of sanctity. Beyond *Malkuth* we have no part or office in the task of preparing the Candidate. I am in correspondence with the final letter *He*.

Celebrant–*Yod, He, Vau, He;* herein and herewith, I communicate to you the Sacred Name which is the synthesis of our research in the Order of the ∴∴. I have come forth from the Sanctuary that is within, bearing the Rosy Cross on my breast. I stand before the Portal of the Second Order as the witness and the messenger thereof. I am the form which the door gives up. I convey the tidings of *Tiphereth*…Truly Honoured Hierophant, give me the Secret Word which is imparted in the Path of *Samech* to those who have entered therein.

Hierophant–**.
Celebrant–**.
Hierophant–**.
Celebrant–**.

Hierophant–The Word is ****, its meaning the Veil of the Tabernacle.

Celebrant–It is the Veil of a Great Mystery, which is revealed to the purified man. By the Secret Word and the Sacred Veil, I declare that the Path is open and the Gate which leads thereto.

Celebrant–ק –.
Hegemon–ק –.
Hiereus–ק –.
Hierophant–ק –.
Celebrant–ק –.
All are seated.
Here ends the Solemn Ceremony of Opening the Temple in the Portal of the Rosy Cross.

THE FIRST POINT
THE RITUAL OF THE 25TH PATH

The Opening of the Door of Samech and the Passage of the Path.

Celebrant–Fratres et Sorores, there is a door which opens from *Tiphereth* and the Grace of the Spheres of Beauty is communicated to the *Sephiroth* that are below. By the power to me entrusted as the Messenger of the Second Order. I have opened that door. Health and benediction, *Fratres*; light from the Rosy Cross; glory from the Sun of *Tephareth*. I testify also that the door opens inward for the reception of those who have been prepared in the outward ways, who carry the grace of the heights in their inmost hearts, who have turned their wills to God. Behold, I come as a Messenger, and my tidings are glad tidings. The time of probation is over; the years of strife are ended; and in all the parts and regions of his natural personality, the dedication of our Honoured *Frater Adveniat Regnum (vel alius)* is complete in the degrees thereof. I have received a dispensation from the Merciful and Exempt Chiefs of the Second Order, seated on the Thrones of *Chesed*, to open the Gate of *Samech*, that he may traverse the 25th Path and receive the annunciation of his election at the Portal of the Rosy Cross.... Honorable *Frater Hegemon*, you have my authority to exercise your office of mediation for the last time in respect of our beloved *Frater Adveniat Regum (vel alius)*; seek him in the precincts without; bring him within the Holy Temple; place him at the western end, facing the Elemental Tables and looking towards the Pillars of the Gate of *Samech* at the Extremity of the *Sephira Yesod*.

The Hegemon–I will show forth tidings of good; I will publish salvation. The ends of the earth shall see it. I will go forth in the brightness thereof, as a lamp that burneth.

He gives the Closing Sign and retires from the Temple. While he is preparing the Philosophus:

Celebrant–*Fratres et Sorores,* may the vivifying rain of the Secret Doctrine refresh us in the wastes of time. May the *Shekinah*, which is an indwelling Glory, bring us with both hands and the Bread of Life. May we pass over the holy hills of incense and sacred mountains of myrrh. May the yoke of the Kingdom be upon us, even the Heavenly Kingdom—the world to come, which is the world of the Holy One.

*The Hedgemon gives the battery of the Portal in the following form—*ףףףף *—. The Sentinel opens the door. The Hegemon enters, leading the Philosophus, who wears the Lamen of admission, but is not hoodwinked, because the four parts of his personality have been consecrated and he is meet to behold the light.*

Hegemon–The Mysteries are a singing voice; let us enter the place of song; let us hearken to the Daughter of the Voice.

Celebrant–He shall enter in peace. The Secret Doctrine is the Tree of Life for those who cultivate it. He shall enter the Kingdom of God. The Law is the Tree of Life. He shall come forth with joy and be welcomed with gladness. The Law is the Waters of Life.

The Hegemon leads the Philosophus to the western side of the Tablets.

Celebrant–*Frater Adveniat Regnum (vel alius)*, I salute you by the Mystic Title of *Pharos Illuminans*, conferred on you in the Grade of *Philosophus*. May your presence be as a tower of light in the presence of your peers. I have come from the secret places through a hidden door, carrying a great dispensation for your advancement in a world unknown. Give me the Symbol which you received in the 4=7 Grade.

Philosophus (who is prompted by the Hegemon)–Master of the Portal, they gave me the Symbol of *Phrath*, which is the fourth river of Eden.

Celebrant–I testify that it is the Path of *Samech*, by which you are called to ascend from the Order of the ∴ ∴ to the threshold of the Second Order. It extends from the Grade of the *Theoricus*, wherein you now stand, to the Holy *Sephira Tiphereth*. Return in your thoughts therein, because of the Path which you must traverse. It is the Path of a River of Light; the Temple is therefore in light; and your eyes are open. If front of you are the four Tablets containing the Divine Names which have been bound about your personality by the consecrations of the Outer Order. In the midst of them there now lies the Tablet of Union. It represents that which binds all the parts of the personality together by a great act of dedication. I now bid you kneel down (*the Philosophus is assisted by the Hegemon*); bow your head reverently; as a token of humility and the turning of the will to God; repeat your sacramental name; and say after me:

THE OBLIGATION

All rise.

Celebrant–I Frater Adveniat Regnum *(vel alius),* most solemnly swear that I will never communicate the secrets of this Path and of the Portal of the Rosy Cross save only in the manner wherein and with the high sanction whereby I her and now receive them. I undertake to maintain the veils between the First and Second Orders. I invoke the four parts of my consecrated personality, the body by which I manifested, the mind which is the seat of consciousness, the emotions and desires which uplift me, and the will which rules in all: may they bear witness to this my pledge. Deal with me in the righteousness of my intention, O just and righteous God. With all the powers of my being, I consecrate and dedicate myself to Thy service in the Grade of the Purified Man. Send down on me, I pray Thee, the light of the spiritual consciousness, that I may be truly enlightened in Thee.

A pause.
Celebrant–Rise, Searcher of the Paths in the Portal of the Rosy Cross.
The Hegemon assists the Philosophus and then retires to his seat.
Celebrant–There is a door which opens outward from each *Sephira*, and on that door is written a Hebrew character. There is a door which opens inward to each *Sephira*, and that door is not inscribed in our system. They who traverse the paths have the right of entrance thereby, if the paths which they follow are lawful. There are three modes of communication upward with *Tiphereth*, but two of the doors are sealed: they open only from within for the descent of influences.
The Hedgemon comes forward with the Lamp—as the sign of fire and light and the sign of the will—raised to his forehead. He pauses at the eastern side of the Tablets and places his Lamp on the Tablet of Union.
Celebrant–Take up the Lamp of the *Hegemon*, who has led you through the Grades of your progress as a minister of mercy and a high priest of redemption. Raise it to your own forehead, to signify the lifting up of the will as an eternal sacrifice.
The Hegemon draws the Philosophus round the Table and places him between the Pillars.
Celebrant— You stand now symbolically at the door of *Samech*, which is the threshold of the 25th Path.... Honourable *Frater Hegemon*, let the *Philosophus* cross the threshold, showing that the door is open.
The Hegemon draws the Philosophus through the Pillars and returns to his seat.
Celebrant–You will now circumambulate the Temple once, proceeding on your path alone, slowly and reverently. Follow the course of the sun; pause as the voices of the Officers are raised in succession to salute you; and at the end of your progress approach the western side of the Altar.
The passage of the 25th Path begins in this manner, and as the *Philosophus* reaches the *Hiereus* on the northern side:

Hiereus–The shadow of the Supernal Hypostases is on you; you have dwelt beneath the wings of the *Shekinah*; you are Israel, who has come out of exile, and the true Gates open to receive you.

As the Philosophus reaches the Celebrant on the eastern side:
Celebrant–Wells of doctrine–deep wells; wells of divine doctrine; wells of love; enter into the wells of doctrine. The study of the doctrine is the work among all works, the worship above all worships, the prayer of all prayers.

As the Philosophus reaches the Hegemon in the South:
Hegemon–The path of spiritual consciousness is the path of the study of the Secret Doctrine. But those who would study the Law must keep it: the Law is understood only in the intercourse of holy union.

As the Philosophus reaches the Hierophant in the West:
Hierophant–Remember, O Pharos Illuminans, that Gate which is the synthesis of all gates, the Grade which is a summary of all Grades; for by such Grade and Gate does man enter into the knowledge of the Holy One.

As the Philosophus still pauses, the Kerux rises, with his Officers, behind the Hierophant.
Kerux—With all the voices of earth and in all its silence, behold, I testify concerning you. Remember that the Divine Word is an eternal holocaust.

The Philosophus passes by the North and so reaches the Altar. The Hedgemon comes forward and receives the Lamp from his hands, which he places on his pedestal and resumes his seat. The Celebrant descends from his Throne and goes to the Altar, where he stands at the eastern side, facing the Philosophus on the West.

Celebrant–Through whatever Grades of our Order the Postulant may pass in this life, they are all differently the stages of his ascent to the height, or otherwise of his return to the centre. The Diagram of the Paths and the *Sephiroth*, which lies before you on the Altar, depicts these stages; but it is also a delineation of the path of descent into manifestation, when the soul had come forth from God.

We are concerned with it, however, in the former aspect, and you will see that the Sephirotic scheme has three chief divisions, corresponding to the Orders in our Fraternity. With the First of them you are already familiar and with the sequence of Grades therein. You stand on the threshold of the Second, corresponding to *Tiphereth*, *Geburah* and *Chesad*, the 5=6 Grade of *Adeptus Minor*, the 6=5 Grade, or that of *Adeptis Major*, and the Exalted Grade of 7=4, being that of the *Adeptus Exemptus*. Above these spheres there is the Supernal Triad, which involves the conception of a Third Order, subsisting in uttermost concealment—like the *Sephiroth* to which it is referred. In symbolical advancement through the Grades and Degrees of our Fraternity, there is no point of entrance thereto or path of communication therewith, except in the Great Mystery of *Daath*. The threefold division which I have mentioned offers a complete analogy with the four worlds of Kabalism. For in *Malkuth* is the world of *Assiah*, to the life of the body corresponds. In *Yetzirah* are *Netzach*, *Hod* and *Yesod*, being the inward parts of the natural man— his will, emotions and mind. *Assiah* and *Yetzirah* are dedicated in the   , which symbolises the conquest of the Edomite Kings. Therefore it is the Kingdom of Israel, the reign of the spirit and of holy souls in *Briah*. Beyond these things there is a world of *Atziluth*.

The Kerux lead the Philosophus to the East.

Celebrant–The Portals which are before you represent all possible modes of egress to the several paths which connect the Grades and *Sephiroth* in the Order of the ∴ ∴ with the *Sephiroth* and the Grades which are beyond. In the North is the Gate of *Mem*, leading from *Hod* to *Geburah*, and to this Path is attributed the 12 Key of the Tarot, that Hanged Man which suggests in strange symbolism the presence of some great mystery. It is one of the vertical Paths, and it is closed for ever to the *Practicus*. In the South is the Gate of *Kaph*, leading from *Netzach* to *Chesed* by another vertical Path, to which is attributed the 13th Key of the Tarot, or that of the Wheel of Fortune. There is no ascent to the heights through this Gate, either in the Outer or Inner Order. There remain for your consideration the 24th, 25th and 26th Paths by which *Tiphereth* is approached from *Netzach*, *Yesod* and *Hod*, or the Grade of *Adeptus Minor* from the Grades which are below. The threshold of this exalted sphere is reached by the vertical Path of *Samech*, which you have just traversed symbolically. The gate by which it was entered is shown here in the East for purposes of convenience, in comparison with the other Gates and Paths. Remember, it was by a vertical Path that you passed from the *Sephira Malkuth* at the beginning of your journey upwards; it is by the corresponding vertical Path that you will now enter the Second Order. The Path of *Tau* is the only vertical Path in the Grades of the ∴ ∴, and it symbolises the making of a good beginning. The pure intention attributed to the *Neophyte* has set him free for the moment from the coiling and uncoiling of the Serpent; though herein also at need are paths of progress. At this entrance or vestibule of the Second Order, you mark a definite and important further stage in your progress, and I commend to you the saving sense of another and a new beginning. See that it is good and true within you, as it is true and holy without, in the world of symbols. So shall you be prepared to follow henceforth the high counsel of the purified life.

The Celebrant draws the Philosophus a little nearer the East.

Celebrant–I must now direct your consideration to the Tarot symbols which stand about the threshold of Adeptship as guardians of the three Paths, communicating with the Grade of *Tiphereth*. By the hypothesis of the Paths and the Tree, it is possible to proceed from the 4=7 Grade of *Netzach* to that of 7=4 in *Chesad*, as it is also from the 3=8 of Hod to the 6=5 of *Geburah*; but these modes of progress are forbidden by the laws of the hierarchy. For this reason the Tarot Keys attributed to the Paths of *Kaph* and *Mem* have no place in the Temple. There remain, however, the 24th, 25th and 26th Paths. But the *Philosophus* cannot enter the

Sephira Tiphereth by the Path of *Nun*, because the Key of Death intervenes.
The Celebrant shows the 13th Tarot Key.
Celebrant–The first meaning lies with utter plainness on the surface of the card, and it does not concern us here. It reminds us, however, of the great truth which is commemorated and symbolised in the Mysteries of all ages and countries— that we must pass ultimately through death to life in the mystical sense. But the time is not yet, nor is the place of the experience here. The 24th Path of the *Sepher Yetzirah* is called the Imaginative Intelligence, and it is said to be the ground of similitude in the likeness of beings and of things. The explanation is that the deep things of spiritual life are in correspondence with life manifested in the material world. Similar bonds of comparison subsist between physical and mystical death; both are a veil, and the curtains in both cases are parted from within, to show that there is life behind. It is unlawful to enter it in either instance by the force of your own act and will. The sealing of the Gate of *Nun* therefore signifies that we must not forestall the experience of mystical death, and the reason is that *Tiphereth* is not the place of resurrection. We must also remember that there is the spiritual death of sin, and this has analogies with an old version of the 13th Tarot Key, in which the skeleton reaps no longer in a grass meadow, but amidst the shadowy flames of *Tophet*. It is the harvest of the second death.
The Celebrant replaces the card and then hands to the Philosophus the 15th Tarot Key.
Celebrant–To enter *Tiphereth* through the left hand or 26th Path is also impossible, as shown by the intervention of the 15th Tarot Key, which is that of Diabolus or Satan, attributed to the Path. In one of its aspects, this is also literally and ritually the symbol of the second death, and to confront it by a forced entrance would be to attempt to attain spiritual life by going down to hell, and by the worship of Satan in the place of God. It would be also as if one should seek to work evil by

good, to enthrone the spirit of denial, and to open the abyss that heaven might be swallowed thereby. The 24th Path of the *Sepher Yetzirah* is called the Renewing Intelligence, and all renovation in the world is said to be operated therewith. We come in this manner to recognise another aspect of the symbol, as a counterpoise to the previous memorials. Satan is also God's emissary; he is life unregenerated, Nature on the lower side, which is red in tooth and claw. He answers to the circle of necessity, blind force, and the bondage represented by the chained figures shown beneath his Altar in the drawing. Remember, O *Frater*, that you are following the path of liberation, but that liberation is according to law. It is for this reason that there is a seal upon the Gate of Ayin, and that seal is not broken. If you begin by keeping the Law, you will end by understanding it. There is much more that might be said to you concerning the forbidden paths to the Portal, but it is part of the knowledge that you will receive in the more inward places of the Second Order.

The Celebrant restores the card to its place and then hands to the Philosophus the 14th Tarot Key.

Celebrant–And now as to the via media, that Path of *Samech* which you have traversed, and wherein the Key of Temperance, the 14th Tarot Key, is discovered for your encouragement and support. It is the way of combination and equilibrium, of providence in desirable change, as for example, in the transit from the material that is without to the spiritual that is within. It is also the principle of sacramental life, the ascent of human nature that the Divine may come down therein. As here depicted, the Key of Temperance is really a synthesis of *Tiphereth* and of the Path which leads thereto. That Path in the *Sepher Yetzirah* is called the Intelligence of Temptation or of Trial, because it is the test of merit which God applies to those whom He calls to His service. The sacred name of *Tiphereth* is bound upon the breast of the figure before you; the star of the Hexagram is beneath it. The splendour of her five-pointed crown is drawn from the five upper *Sephiroth* that are below. She is the symbol of the purified life in spiritual consciousness, and he that has attained thereto shall draw, my brother, all the parts of his personality into the redemption of the higher nature. This is illustrated by Zoharic tradition, which says that the letter *Samech* receives increase from *Binah*, so that it may raise up the fallen *Sephiroth*, including *Malkuth*.

The Hegemon comes up to the Philosophus. The Celebrant returns to his Throne, and, standing thereat, continues:

Celebrant–Fratres et Sorores, it is within ourselves, and so only, that the *Sephiroth* which fell in us are in us also raised; and seeing that in the progress of our mystery we leave *Malkuth* to abide for a season in *Tiphereth*, it is indubitable that we take the lower *Sephiroth* into exaltation. And so all things shall be one, for the immemorial miracle of the one great work of the soul. Unto which I pray that we who have been of old elected, seeing that we are also chosen, may be dedicated now and henceforward, world without end.

The Celebrant resumes his seat.

Celebrant—Honourable *Frater Hegemon*, you have my command to lead our beloved *Frater* to the courts of the Temple. He has traversed the Path of *Samech*, and the secrets appertaining to the Portal will be communicated on his return.

The Philosophus is led out accordingly, and is left in the vestibule. The Hegemon re-enters the Temple.

Here ends the First Point.

THE SECOND POINT
THE PORTAL OF TIPHERETH

On returning to the Temple, the Hegemon proceeds to his seat, and, standing thereat, facing East, he say:

Hegemon–Lord, now lettest Thou Thy servants depart in peace, for our eyes have seen Thy salvation in the union of *Tiphereth* and *Malkuth*.

Celebrant–To the glory of Thine elect, world without end; in the light which is perfect love; and this is the love of perfection.

The Officers of the Outer Order disrobe and put away their vestments. Their seats are removed, and they mingle with the ordinary members. The pedestal is taken from before the Throne of the East. The Pillars are set on each side of the Throne. The Lamp of the Hegemon now burns on the Tablet of Union. The Philosophus is led in by the Hegemon, who wears the crossed Ribbons of the Outer and Inner Orders, but no other insignia. The Philosophus is seated in the West before the Tablets, facing the Throne of the East.

Celebrant–There is a door in *Tiphereth* which shall open for you, my brother; the emblazonment of visible letters does not appear thereon, yet it is full of spiritual inscriptions. My Throne is between the Pillars thereof, and I symbolise the opening of the Gate. In this sense I am the Gate and Way of your advancement. May it be unto you the Door of Conversion, the Portal and Path of Heaven. Through a period of probation and of patience, of reflection in the heart upon the Paths so far travelled, O *Frater Pharos Illuminans*, you have reached this point in your journey, and here is the dividing of the veil. You stand now before the Portal of the Adepts, and you have entered it by that middle way which, as you were told in the 4=7 Grade, is the path of return into unity. It was said to you in that Grade: the rending of the darkness is at hand. You took up your cross as directed and went in search of the light. It is in this manner that you came to the Gate of *Samech*, and there–speaking symbolically–you have laid down the cross for the moment, receiving, in the *Lamen* which you wear, another title of admission; it shall be unto you a Sign of the Rending, a sign that the Wings of the Morning are uplifted in the Orient of Life. You will observe that in this *Lamen* the Four Living Creatures of Ezekiel are grouped together in consonance with the inward meaning of your progress through the Grades of the ∴ ∴. Leo at the summit signifies the Grade of *Philosophus* and the purification of your natural will. The Bull at the lowermost point represents *Malkuth* and the consecration of your earthly body. The Man corresponds to *Yesod*, the Grade of *Theoricus* and the purification of your material mind. The Eagle has reference to *Hod*, to the 3=8 of *Practicus*, and to the human emotions and desires which are hallowed therein. The white ribbon from which the *Lamen* depends signified the consecration of your entire personality. You enter, therefore, also in virtue of purity. The Four Living Creatures correspond in *Zoharic* tradition to the Angels of the four quarters and to the Divine Names emblazoned thereon. We learn also that the four elements, of which man is symbolically made–which were gathered by the *Elohim* from the four quarters of heaven, and correspond to the parts of our personality–are ruled in obedience to those who obey the Law, or in other words that man is detached by sanctity from the bondage of the elements. In conclusion as to this matter, the *Lamen* which you wear offers certain analogies with that of the *Hiereus* in the Grades of the ∴ ∴. That is also a Sign of the rending, the Sacred Triad of Light formulated in the void of the darkness. It is further a synthesis of the Paths which stand about the Portal of the Adepts. I have said that you have laid down the cross at the threshold of the Gate of *Samech*, but this is a for a period only; it is again to be taken up, and it is now shown to you in the East, reposing on the breast of the Messenger who has come to you from the Grades beyond. I am sealed with the Rosy Cross, and you should know that the Rose in its highest understanding is the Divine principle operating in humanity and in you, so that sins which are scarlet may become whiter than snow and that the whiteness of your purified life may be incarnadined by Divine Fire. How is that Fire communicated? It is by the operation of the Secret Doctrine, the students of which are compared in our tradition to roses, in which sense the Rose is the Israel of God. More generally, the Rose is also the Elect and the thorns are that world of humanity which is without the Sanctuary of the chosen ones. The five petals correspond to the five virtues which lead to perfection; these virtues are mystic paths; and they are five manner of wounding by which the Adept is crucified to himself and to the world for the manifestation of the Divine within him. The Rose is also a chalice, and it Mystery, the Mystery of the Ruby Rose, is that of the Chalice of Salvation. It is lastly the Cup of Benedictions; and these modes of interpretation, with many others, their seeming divergence notwithstanding, are one at the root, as a rose with many blossoms springing from a single stem.

The Cross which I bear has analogies with the *Lamen* of a *Hierophant*, which–even as the Rosy Cross–summarises at a very high point the Secret Doctrine of the Second Birth and establishes its analogy with birth in the natural order. It is consciousness opening into the Divine. Except in a secondary sense and in lower degrees, the Rose does not symbolise the material desires immolated on the cross of suffering; it is a symbol of the Beautific Vision which only unfolds on the cross, though it is formulated in the Outer Order from very far away. Those who attain this vision, thereby and thereon, bow their heads and say: It is finished.... But this is the withdrawn state in which consciousness enters the Absolute.

You should understand further that the Vision, as the Banner of the East exhibits, is formulated on the background of purity. It is the simplicity and singleness and detachment and continence concerning which it may be said that he who is sealed therewith shall be opened to Divine things in the universe, even as the Lamb slain from the foundation of the world opened the Book of Life.

Love and understanding are the motive, the secret and the harmony of that world.

We have spoken to you of many hallowings, and I invite you more especially at this stage to remember the turning of the will, which is the deeper meaning of its consecration in the Grade of *Philosophus*. This is the sense in which the Sons and Daughters of the Doctrine, who have become familiar by experience with the Mysteries of the Way, the Truth and the Life, are declared to be little children—that is to say, at the beginning of their initiation. They have graduated in conformity, in the union of the human with the Divine will, which is the earnest of the ineffable union. It is the condition of the opening of the eyes, so that the eyes see and the heart realises the Eternal Object of research.

What was it that dawned upon the soul in the *Neophyte* Grade? The blind sense of want, a great desire, the sense of want, a longing for reality, the consciousness of darkness, and the first suggestion of twilight before morning. The path of search became a path of dedication, and that dedication has brought you to the threshold of higher light, where, in place of the desire of the spirit, you should enter into some realisation of the consciousness thereof.

As a Lord of the Paths, you have traversed the Path of Temperance. Take up the Lamp which reposes now in the centre of the Tablet of Union. *(This is done by the Philosophus.)* Raise it again to your forehead. *(This should be done by the Philosophus, following the course of the sun and without the help of a guide.)* Place the Lamp upon the Altar. Retire into your inward self, and so depose your dedicated human will on the Supernal Altar of Burnt Offerings before the Divine Will.

The Celebrant rises with uplifted arms.

Celebrant–O Frater Pharos Illuminans, The Lord Himself enlighten thee. This is thine offering. The Lord thy God accept thee. This is conformity.

The Celebrant resumes his seat.

Celebrant–It is by such sacrifice that those who are called to the knowledge on this earth of the Life of life become elect thereto; those who are chosen become heirs at law, and the heirs enter into their heritage. You have now made your offering on the threshold of the Inner Temple. This is the Court of its Tabernacle. The years of strife are ended. I have prayed for peace in all your habitations; the price is paid. May the peace that is signed in heaven be declared also on earth. The time of probation is over. I have come through a gate of peace; behold, I have come quickly, lest your steps should err in the paths. Come hither. The door is behind me. I have opened the ways thereto; you shall enter and go in.

The Celebrant by a gesture causes the Philosophus to approach his Throne in the East.

Celebrant–May you enter into the practice of the presence of God, by which you will attain the consciousness of God in the spirit, of God Who is within. Let your heart be filled with holy expectation, and you shall hear in a high symbolism the Divine Voice speaking in the universe and the Christ spirit giving testimony concerning itself and concerning the path of your attainment.

The Celebrant rises and still standing on the dais of his Throne.

Celebrant–By the power in me vested as the Master of the Portal, I declare that the veil is parted and I give you the Sign of its Rending. Stretch forth your hands in front of you, with the palms outward, as in the act of dividing a veil or setting curtains aside.

The Celebrant communicates the Sign.

Celebrant–This is the answering Sign. Let your hands be raised higher and separated widely thus, with the palms turned inward. Then bring the hands together, as in the act of drawing up curtains and closing them.

The Celebrant communicates the Closing Sign.

Celebrant–These are the Pass-Signs from the First to the Second Order, and the Secret Word is * *,* *,* *,* *–that is to say, * * * *, meaning the Veil of the Tabernacle. It is exchanged by the separate letters. Follow me therefore, thus:
Celebrant–* *.
Philosophus (who is prompted by the Celebrant)–* *.
Celebrant–* *.
Philosophus (who is prompted)–* *.

Celebrant–I invest you with the Ribbon of the Second Order, which is white bordered with gold; the symbols of the 5=6 Grade are emblazoned thereon, with the numbers of the 24th, 25th and 26th Paths, by which *Tiphereth* is approached from three of the *Sephiroth* that are beneath it. The Ribbon is worn over the left shoulder opposite to that of the Order of the ∴ ∴. It is worn crosswise therewith in the Outer Temple; it shows that you have opened the Gate of *Samech* and have been admitted to the Portal of the Adepts.

The Celebrant takes the hand of the Philosophus and draws him round so that he faces to the West.

Celebrant–To all who have entered that Portal; to the Fratres et Sorores in all Grades of Adeptship, I proclaim that the Honoured *Frater Adveniat Regnum (vel alius)* is a Lord of the 24th, 25th and 26th Paths and that he stands on the threshold of *Tiphereth*.

The Celebrant resumes his seat.

Celebrant–You will now take your place among the Brethren of the Second Order in the East of the Temple.

The Philosophus is directed accordingly, and when he is seated:

Celebrant–*Fratres et Sorores*, when the Veil of the Tabernacle is parted by reverend and holy hands moving from within, the Holy Voice says unto each in this Order: Come in peace. The offices of our Temple are therefore offices of mercy, reflected from the Supreme Crown. *Kether* is the world of mercy, the place where there is neither sorrow nor wrath, neither separateness, but glory and splendour, strength and joy. It is also supernal loving-kindness, which is communicated to *Chokmah*, and *Chokmah* is the beginning and the end, the door by which there is entrance to the King of Heaven. It is good pleasure and benevolence, and in the *Sephira Chesed* it passes into manifested love. But by *Chesed* the world was made and all the *Sephiroth* beneath are saturated with benignity therefrom. The Four Worlds of *Kabalism* are therefore worlds of love, and the Grades of the Second Order, which correspond in our symbolism with the world of *Briah*, are the palaces thereof: holiness, love, the works by which we are judged, the good will that consecrates works, the Divine intention which is their substance, the repose that remains for all who have turned to God in their hearts, the purity which is the quintessence of moral life, and God as all in all. But this is perfection. Hereof is the prospect before you, *O Frater Adveniat Regnum*. You are in search of the secret, that Stone of the Wise which we pray to attain in this Temple, the Stone which transmutes those whom it does not break. That White Stone, the true Medicine thereof and the Divine Tincture are in our inward nature. Was it not said to you of old that God is within? When the Seven Gifts of the Divine Spirit are declared in the consciousness—then is the secret found. This is the Doctrine of Light, and where is that Light, my Brother? Our tradition tells us that it is in the holy angles of the Cross, and this is an allegory of our lower nature, that work to which you are called henceforth. Innocent of hands and clean of heart, you will go up the Mountain of the Lord by the following of that Path. Remember the Temple on its summit and the aspiration of the Sons and Daughters of Desire which beat about its Golden Gates. This is the last message which I give from the Throne of the Portal: it takes us where we should always be in spirit—to the Throne of God. But, *Fratres et Sorores*, and all ye chosen hearts—this is *Atziluth*.

Here ends the Ceremony of Admission to the Portal of the Rosy Cross.

THE HIGH OFFICE OF CLOSING THE HOLY PORTAL

Celebrant—Fratres et Sorores, assist me to close the Holy Temple according to the Ritual of the 25th Path and in the Grade appertaining to the Portal of the Rosy Cross.

All rise.

He descends from his Throne and faces East with arms extended in the opening Sign of the Grade.

Celebrant–I have entered, O Merciful Father, behind the Veil of the Tabernacle. I have seen the glorious Sun of *Tiphereth*. But I know that there is another splendour, another light, another and more glorious Sun. O after all the radiance of the natural world, after the golden dawn and the noonday splendour, give us Thine own light, the true illumination that is within, even the Sun of Thy truth, the inexpressible splendour of Thy Presence, and the glory of Thy perfect Union.

The Celebrant returns to his Throne and remains standing.

Celebrant–Fratres et Sorores, I declare that the Word is * * * * and that its meaning is the Veil of the Tabernacle.

He gives the Closing Sign.

Celebrant–In and by that Word, and in accordance with the Mystic Sign, I close this Holy Temple.

He gives the Battery of the Grade.

Here ends the Ritual of the Portal of the Rosy Cross.

APPENDIX III

INNER ORDER STUDY CURRICULM OF THE GOLDEN DAWN

ZELATOR ADEPTUS MINOR – DOCUMENTS RECEIVED
Stage One
1. Admission Ceremony, after which receive Ritual A (General Instructions). Adeptus Minor Ritual is to be studied thoroughly, especially the clauses of the Obligation.
2. Receive Ritual of the Pentagram and commit to memory.
3. Receive Ritual of the Hexagram and commit to memory.
4. Receive Ritual U, the Microcosm, to be attentively studied, though not learned by heart.
5. Receive Ritual Z1 and Z3.
6. Receive Ritual D and make Lotus Wand, to be consecrated after approval of Chief in Charge.
7. Receive Ritual E and F, and make Rose Cross, and consecrate it after approval as before.
8. Receive Ritual G and consecrate the 5 Implements as before.
9. Receive Ritual K, and the Consecration Ceremony, and M, the Hermes Vision and the Lineal Figures; also W Hodos Chamelionis.
10. Receive and study Flying Rolls 1-10 inclusive, at any period during the First Stage.
(The Adept must pass Examination marked A and B at the end of the First Stage, thus becoming a Zelator Adeptus Minor).
Stage Two
11. Receive and study Flying Rolls 11, 12, 14, 20, 21, 28, 29, and may now pass C, G, and E examinations.

Stage Three
12. Receive and study Rituals N, O, P, Q, R. Must now pass G, C, D and E examinations. (Tarot Study)
Stage Four
13. Receive and study rituals H, S, T, X, Y. Must now pass F examination.
Stage Five
14. Receive and study Z2 Rituals, and practice Consecration and Invocation. Practical success in Ceremony of Z2 is required.

ZELATOR ADEPTUS MINOR- EXAMINATION PROCEDURES
A. PRELIMINARY (Written and Vocal)
1. Be familiar with all clauses of the Obligation, Minutum Mundum Diagrams, Names, Letters, Colours and Tarot associations to Sephiroth and Paths.
2. Draw sigil from Rose Cross for any given name.
3. Supreme Ritual of Pentagram, allotment of Elements, Names and Forces; mode of drawing any or all. Note: Effect must be shown as well as verbal accuracy.

B. ELEMENTARY (Written and Vocal)
4. The Magical Implements: their construction, constitution, symbolism and rules for use. The dangers of imperfect constructions and ignorant use of. Ceremonies of Consecration: Formulae of Invocation.

C. PSYCHIC (Written and Vocal)
5. Describe results of impressions of supplied Symbols of Tattwas.

D. DIVINATION (Written)
6. A Divination question (to be supplied by Chief) divined through Astrology, Geomancy and Tarot. Note: On each occasion the same question will be asked but will be worded differently.

E. MAGIC
7. Talismans and Flashing Tablets: their formulation and consecration.
8. Formation of Angelic and Telesmatic Figures from Letters of Name supplied. Use of Figures when ascending to the Planes.

Mode of vibration Divine Names using ADONAI HA ARETZ until radiance of aura is established.
9. Perform Ceremony of Invocation or Banishing of the forces of any given Sign, Planet or Element.
10. Make and consecrate a talisman for a given purpose. Make and charge three Flashing Tablets, viz: for an Element, Planet and Sign. Draw and colour Angelic figures or Elemental figures appropriate to these may be required.

F. ELEMENTAL ENOCHIAN TABLETS
11. Study all associations to each square in a complete lesser angle until one can tell at a glance what these associations are from any angle of any board.
12. Draw and color Sphinx of any Serviant Square as required.

G. SYMBOLICAL (Written and Vocal)
13. Explain all allusions to any paragraph and symbolism of any Robe, Lamen, Wand or Action of the Neophyte Ritual, including Coptic Alphabet and Secret Words.
14. Perform the Z2 Ritual or Evocation and Consecration before Examiner.

Preliminary Notes: General Orders H
Each Th.A.M. shall make, adapt, or consecrate by himself the Ring and Disk of a Theoricus for use in Divination and Consultation. The same Ring, or similar, is to be worn as a badge of his Grade, suspended from a ribbon of one, or of all four colours of Malkuth.

He or she shall carefully study and practice the following subjects, in which a rigid examination will have to be passed before the Grade of Practicus Adeptus Minor can be obtained.
1. A careful study of the symbolism contained in the Zelator Ritual of the First Order, so as to be able to explain any part thereof. A lecture on this subject will be available.
2. A development of the Sense of Clairaudience in the Spirit Vision.
3. The knowledge of the Ritual of the 12 gates in Skrying and Travelling in the Spirit Vision, answering to the diagram of the Table of Shewbread.

4. The method of Bringing the Divine White Brilliance into Action by a certain Ritual of Ascent and Descent.
5. Careful and elaborate study and analysis and the four squares above the Calvary Crosses in each Less Angle of the Four Enochian Tablets, and their influence when combined with the Serviant Squares of each Lesser Angle.
6. Development of the employment and uses of Telemata and Symbols.
7. Of the combination of diverse forces so as to reconcile their action in the same symbol of Telesma.
8. The Egyptian Art of the Formation of a combined series of images of Gods or Forces, so as to have the effect of continuous Prayer or Invocation for the Power desired.
9. The knowledge of ShDIALchi or the Art of taking, in any working, the godform which would govern the same, by means of identification with a Telesmatic figure.
10. The True system of Astrological Divination.
11. Of the Correspondence existing between each of the 16 figures of Geomancy, and each of the Lesser Angles of the Enochian Tablets treated as a whole.
12. Tarot Divination translated into Magical Action.
13. The Knowledge of the Secret Ritual of the symbolism of the order of the Days of the Week of Creation, answering to the Diagram of the Seven-Branched Candlestick.
14. The thorough elementary knowledge of the Formulas of the Awakening of the Abodes, by means of the Play or Raying of the Checkers of the Lesser Angles of the Enochian Tablets.
15. The opening of the knowledge of the Masculine and Feminine Potencies necessary unto the manifestation of all things symbolised in the Diagram of the Flaming Sword between **METATRON** and **SANDALPHON**.

Author's Note: Though the wording of the Theoricus Adeptus Minor Curriculum varies slightly from other published copies, in essence it is much the same. This Grade was never implemented at Whare Ra, though Felkin had copies of both the Th.A.M. Grade structure outlines.

APPENDIX IV

"THE ORDER OF THE ROUND TABLE"

by Jack Taylor

(known also as "The Order of the Cross and Sword")

The roots of this Order go far back into antiquity long before Christianity which came to Britain in A.D. 36, when a company of twelve led by St. Joseph of Arimathea arrived to establish the first Christian Church and community in Britain. It was founded long before the life time of King Arthur, who, when in his turn had become Grandmaster, brought the Order out from under the veil of secrecy it had previously been functioning under and established it as a powerful force for righteousness in the public and outer world.

Historians agree that this re-establishment of the Order of the Round Table took place in 462 A.D.

The main object of the Round Table Fellowship under the Grandmastership of King Arthur was to bring as much of the Christian Ideals as the people could assimilate into the public life and activities of his time. The laws of true chivalry were laid down and they became the foundation of all that is best in European Civilization.

Following the death of King Arthur there were times when the Order flourished exceedingly. In the Crusades of 1250 A.D. between five and six hundred knights went to Palestine. Near Accra all but a certain Sir Hugo were killed.

The Order was reconstituted by Sir Hugo after his eventual return from the Crusades whereat so many knights were slain.

Following on from this there were times when the Order dwindled down to only one representative, and this happened when the 37th Grandmaster, Neville Meakin (Tudor) was an infant. The Reverend Meakin adopted the boy and brought him up as his own son. It was not until young Neville came of age at that same time handed him the family papers and gave him instruction in regard to the Order. Neville was so attached to his foster father that he preferred to retain the name Meakin. Neville Meakin received his Grandmastership by descendency from the original Sir Mordred who was said to have been a cousin of King Arthur.

Neville was introduced to Doctor and Mrs. Felkin by a mutual friend in 1909. He had taken a double first at Oxford University but was then suffering from tuberculosis from which he never fully recovered. When Dr. and Mrs. Felkin first met him Neville had come to the conclusion that marriage was not for him. Their friendship had developed rapidly and it was inevitable that Dr. Felkin should have been his first choice in extending the Order. He invested the Doctor with the various degrees of the Order up to that of "Mage" and eventually appointed Dr. Felkin as his successor to the Grandmastership of the Order.

There were living in 1910 three members of the Tudor Family all being "Knights of the King's household" (Neville had been knighted in 1897 and Plantaganet–an American son–in 1908), constituting a quorum which made it possible to reorganise the Order and set it upon a wider footing. Neville died in the arms of Dr. Felkin in October, 1912.

Dr. Felkin F.R.C.S. (Edin.) was a distinguished physician, scientist and explorer. He was a member of the Royal Geographical Society, the Anthropological Society, the Ethnographical Society, as well as of corresponding societies on the Continent. He was also a Mason of the 33rd degree, a Knight Templar, a leading member of the Anti-Slavery Society and on the Medical Staff of London National Guard. He was definitely a Christian man.

There was a prophecy in the Order that the Order would at some time be taken across the seas to certain islands where it would again flourish.

In 1912 Dr. Felkin, the 41st Grandmaster of the Order, justified the first part of this prophecy and brought to New Zealand the symbols and teachings of the Order in preparation for the foundation of the Order in New Zealand. The Doctor believed that the Order should be kept very much alive at all costs and gave his very life to this end.

Mr. Reginald Gardiner and his wife had established their home in Havelock North and were soon joined by a stranger who knocked at their door. The stranger was duly welcomed and these three people thereafter began naturally to work in a harmony of action the ultimate purpose of which they sensed rather than could define. These "beginnings" were the Arts and Crafts Association in 1908. They had a feeling that they were working in expectation of something that they felt but could not define. They called their magazine the "Forerunner."

A Church of England mission visited Hawke's Bay. The missioner was a man of deep spiritual understanding and saw in the work of these "forerunners" the preparation for a greater purpose. He stated to the effect "You have done well. Now I will send you from England the people who will raise the house upon the foundations you have laid."

Following the mission, in 1912, Dr. Felkin and his wife and daughter arrived in Havelock North and placed his proposals before the little band of Forerunners. He told them that they had been laying the foundations of a spiritual work of immeasurable consequence, and that with their consent he would establish two secret schools:–A school of Christian spiritual wisdom, and a school of Christian Chivalry–the Order of the Table Round.

The Order of the Table Round began in New Zealand as a small group at first, but others were attracted who believed in the ideals of Christian Chivalry and who set to work to try to practice them and to spread them through the National Life.

Early in 1914 Andrew Hamilton Russell, consequent upon the death of Dr. Felkin, was elected and installed as the second Grandmaster of the O.T.R. in New Zealand but following the outbreak of World War I in August of that year and his departure from New Zealand on Active Service, and in anticipation of a lengthy absence abroad, he resigned the office and Mr. Reginald Gardiner was installed as Grandmaster in his place.

The above notes have been culled from "A History of the Order of the Table Round," written in 1962, a copy whereof, together with two leaflets, one "The Spirit of Chivalry," giving the prayer issued by the "Society of men who are working to restore the spirit of Christian chivalry in our Nation" and the Litany which are copied below, and the other "The Chivalric Society, What it is and what it does," have been kindly made available to this writer, for his perusal and use in this work, by a Senior member of long standing in the O.T.R. To him I express my sincere thanks for this courtesy.

The extracts from the latter leaflet follow:

"It is not widely known because for hundreds of years it has chosen to work under an obligation of silence. This requires its members to try to express the Chivalric ideal in deeds rather than in words.

The Chivalric ideal is aptly summed up in the form of obligation which its members used to take—I pledge my word to use such strength of mind and body as the Most High bestows upon me, for the helping of the weak, who do in any wise need help for the righting of the wrong in every way."

"So, at the Physical level some members work in other Service Organisations and in other ways. At the Mental and Spiritual levels, by giving such counsel and comfort as they can IF ASKED; and by praying for the sick or those in need, or for various causes where such help has been solicited.

"Finally we ask you to respect our desire to remain anonymous and to work in silence, by not discussing the Order or its members with others, unless you think it might help another to told about it."

THE PRAYER

"We pray, O Lord, that Thou wilt so reveal Thyself to us, that through us, men may be drawn to the love of Thee.

That Thou wilt give us the gifts of Galilee, the gifts of gaiety and freedom and simplicity to make our tired world grow young again,

That Thou wilt pour Thy spirit more and more into the life of men; giving us clean laughter and good sportsmanship, kindness, generosity and gentleness, honour, courtesy, and self-control.

That Thou wilt reveal Thyself in fellowship; that a world, which rests on competition, may learn from Thee the nature of the Father, and by the power of Thy Spirit live in love according to His will,

That Thou wilt inspire science, art, and letters, to be the expression of God through human skill,

That Thou wilt consecrate the aspirations of the young and the rebellious; and strengthen the prophets that they may be forerunners of Thy kingdom,

That Thou wilt give such power to Thy Church that she may have life and life more abundantly, with courage to go forward daringly, trusting in Thy leadership, and unfettered by the past.

Amen."

New Falcon Publications
**Publisher of Controversial Books and CDs
Invites You to Visit Our Website:
http://www.newfalcon.com**

At the Falcon website you can:

- Browse the online catalog of all our great titles, including books by Robert Anton Wilson, Christopher S. Hyatt, Israel Regardie, Aleister Crowley, Timothy Leary, Osho, Lon Milo DuQuette and many more
- Find out what's available and what's out of stock
- Get special discounts
- Order our titles through our secure online server
- Find products not available anywhere else including:
    - One of a kind and limited availability products
    - Special packages
    - Special pricing
- And much, much more

Get online today at http://www.newfalcon.com